Celebrating
THE
RESURRECTION

J. Michael Shannon & Robert C. Shannon

**SERMONS,
OUTLINES,
ILLUSTRATIONS,
MEDITATIONS, AND
PROGRAM IDEAS**

 STANDARD PUBLISHING
Cincinnati, Ohio   3021

Sharing the thoughts of his own heart, the author may express views that are not entirely consistent with those of the publisher.

Library of Congress Cataloging in Publication Data

Shannon, J. Michael.
  Celebrating the Resurrection.

    1. Easter service.   I. Shannon, Robert, 1930-
II. Title.
BV55.S48   1984   263'.93   83-18174
ISBN 0-87239-754-8

CONTENTS

WORSHIP RESOURCES

PREACHING RESOURCES

PROGRAM RESOURCES

**WORSHIP
RESOURCES**

CALLS TO WORSHIP

Hear . . . O Lord, attend unto my cry; give ear unto my prayer.   Psalm 17:1

Give ear, O Shepherd of Israel, thou that leadest Joseph like a flock; thou that dwellest between the cherubim, shine forth.
                                                   Psalm 80:1

The Lord liveth; and blessed be my Rock; and let the God of my salvation be exalted.   Psalm 18:46

Hear my cry, O God; attend unto my prayer. From the end of the earth will I cry unto thee.   Psalm 61:1, 2

Come and see the works of God. . . . Come and hear, all ye that fear God.   Psalm 66:5, 16

O praise the Lord, all ye nations: praise him, all ye people. For his merciful kindness is great toward us: and the truth of the Lord endureth forever. Praise ye the Lord.   Psalm 117

As the hart panteth after the water brooks, so panteth my soul after thee, O God. My soul thirsteth for God, for the living God.   Psalm 42:1, 2

Great is the Lord, and greatly to be praised; and his greatness is unsearchable.   Psalm 145:3

O Lord, our Lord, how excellent is thy name in all the earth!
                                                     Psalm 8:1

> O for a thousand tongues to sing
> My great Redeemer's praise,
> The glories of my God and King,
> The triumphs of His grace!
>
> Charles Wesley

7

The Lord of hosts is with us; the God of Jacob is our refuge.
Psalm 46:7, 11

The Lord is my portion, saith my soul; therefore will I hope in him. The Lord is good unto them that wait for him, to the soul that seeketh him.
Lamentations 3:24, 25

The Lord is in his holy temple, the Lord's throne is in heaven: his eyes behold, his eyelids try, the children of men.
Psalm 11:4

O magnify the Lord with me, and let us exalt His name together.
Psalm 34:3

And the four beasts . . . rest not day and night, saying, Holy, holy, holy, Lord God Almighty, which was, and is, and is to come.
Revelation 4:8

The Lord is my light and my salvation; whom shall I fear? The Lord is the strength of my life; of whom shall I be afraid?
Psalm 27:1

O give thanks unto the Lord: for he is good; for his mercy endureth for ever. O give thanks unto the God of heaven: for his mercy endureth for ever.
Psalm 136:1, 26

Let all the earth fear the Lord: let all the inhabitants of the world stand in awe of him. For he spake, and it was done; he commanded and it stood fast.
Psalm 33:8, 9

STEWARDSHIP MEDITATIONS

If we were to worship without giving, we would be the first people in history and the only people in the world to do so! The pagan brings an offering to his idol. The Psalms urged the Jews to "bring an offering" and come into the courts of the temple. Jesus sat by the treasury as worshipers cast in their gifts. Paul urged Christians to prepare an offering. Surely, we would not want to be the first to attempt worship without giving!

We must not misunderstand that old hymn "Rock of Ages." It is the favorite of some because of the verse that begins, "Nothing in my hand I bring!" Is that our theme song? It refers to the basis of our forgiveness—not to the acts of our worship. It is true that no offering of ours can take away sin. "Jesus paid it all." It is also true that no real gratitude exists apart from the desire to give, to bring an offering!

"If money talks, as some folks tell, to most of us it says, 'Farewell!' " When your money talks, does it say, "Praise God, from whom all blessings flow?" Does it say "Thank you, Lord, for saving my soul?" When your money talks, what does it say?

In the entire history of this earth, only about 8,500 tons of gold have been produced. The metal is so dense that all of the gold ever seen on earth could be contained in a cube eighteen yards on each side! Yet people will steal for it, kill for it, live for it, die for it! Giving keeps us from letting money become our master, or letting gold be our god.

Tourism is the principal means of livelihood on the Caribbean island of Aruba. Aruba means "land of gold," but no gold was ever found there. What a disappointment that must have been to the early explorers. Does our stewardship hold out great promise and then prove to be empty? Is God disappointed in our stewardship?

9

No man can open the windows of heaven, but God can and does. He promised in Malachi 3:10 to open them for every man who would be faithful to Him by bringing the whole tithe into His house. Thousands have proved the promise true. He wants to open the windows of heaven for you. He wants to pour out the best blessings upon you. But He waits to see whether you believe the promise enough to obey the command.

A little boy was asked the meaning of stewardship. He said, "Life is like a great ship loaded with cargo to be delivered to many different people in many different places. I am the captain. God is the owner!"

Giving is an act of faith. We give, believing that God will provide for our needs. We give, believing that Christ's church is worthy of our offerings. We give, believing that men are lost. We give, believing that the gospel can save them. If you do not give, which of these do you disbelieve?

St. Peter's is not the only great church in Rome. The church of St. Mary Major is a grand cathedral with a high, vaulted ceiling. The ceiling is covered with gold—real gold! It is the *first* gold that Columbus brought back from the New World. We are impressed that the *first* gold was given to God. That's what He wants all of us to do—put Him first!

Not everyone gives in proportion to what he possesses. Not everyone gives in proportion to what he earns. Not everyone gives in proportion to the way he has been blessed. But everyone is a proportion giver. We all give in proportion to the amount of religion we really have!

A lady gave a coin to a beggar saying, "That's more than God ever gave me." "No," said the beggar, "God gave you all you have." "No," said the lady, "He only loaned it to me so that I could distribute it for Him."

Since the dawn of time, man has worshiped by making sacrifices. On the very edge of Eden, men made offerings to God. We stand here in a long, long line of ancient tradition. And from the beginning to the present the bringing of these

10

offerings has been seen as an act of worship, hallowed and sacred!

It actually happened in a Sunday School class of boys long ago. The teacher asked each lad to quote a Bible verse as the offering was taken. One said, "The Lord loveth a cheerful giver." Another said, "Blessed is he that considereth the poor." A third boy blurted out, "A fool and his money are soon parted." The world says you are a fool to give. God says you are a fool *not* to give!"

A man named his boat "Mama's Mink." The meaning is obvious. If we were frank, would some have to name their boats "God's Tenth?" Would some have to name their cars "God's Tenth?" Would some have to name their houses "God's Tenth?"

Ninety percent of all the flowers in the world have an unpleasant odor or no odor at all. Yet, we remember the flowers because of the ten percent that are pleasantly fragrant! Ten percent that is given is remembered long after we have forgotten how we spent the ninety percent. The ten percent rises as "an odor of a sweet savor to God."

✈ Everything Midas touched turned to gold. He thought it was a blessing. He found it to be a curse. His food turned to gold. His child turned to gold. Here we see the reverse of the Midas touch. God turns our gold into truth and comfort; into a voice proclaiming the good news; into a hand helping the sick; into a force striking free the chains of sin; into life everlasting. We bring our money so that He may transform it into something *truly* valuable.

COMMUNION MEDITATIONS

Some of the streets of Mexico City are named after significant events in Mexican history. There is a Fifth of September Street, a Tenth of September Street, and a Twentieth of November Street. Thus they hope to keep in Mexican memory the significant events of their past. The gospel writers do not even bother to record the date of the crucifixion. There is even some disagreement on the day of the week of the crucifixion! Why didn't the Biblical writers fix the date with accuracy?

The answer is that God did not want an annual observance but a weekly observance. He did not want us to come to this table once a year but once a week. Every Lord's Day we have an appointment here. And we are to remember not just the day but the events of that day. The events of crucifixion and resurrection!

Just after the crucifixion, you find the disciples meeting in secret behind closed doors—afraid. A few days later, you find them preaching openly in synagogue and marketplace—unafraid. What made the difference? A meeting with Jesus in the locked upper room.

So we come to our "upper room" filled with fears and anxieties. And if we meet Christ here, we lose them all—and go out to face tomorrow unafraid. He has promised to meet us here. Let us keep our appointment with Him—now.

"I have finished the work which thou gavest me to do" (John 17:4). And then from the cross, a shout of triumph. The mound builders left behind no unfinished work. Raphael left an unfinished painting and Hayden an unfinished symphony; but those ancient inhabitants of our continent, who lived before the American Indian, left behind no unfinished work. The mounds that dot Ohio and the Midwest are monuments to their perseverance and ambition and energy. A greater work was Christ's; but He could say on the cross, "It is finished!" The Lord's Supper is a monument to this completed work of Christ.

Christ walked with two along the Emmaus road, after the resurrection, and they did not know that it was He. But He accepted their invitation to come into their home and sat down with them for the evening meal; and when prayer was offered and the bread broken, THEN their eyes were opened and they knew who Christ was. He was known to them in the breaking of bread. So He is known to us here—in the breaking of bread.

✝ "Forasmuch as ye know that ye were not redeemed with corruptible things as silver and gold, . . . but with the precious blood of Christ" (1 Peter 1:18, 19). The visitor to old Saint Augustine in Florida is shown the city's ancient slave market. It is disturbing to think of the thousands of men and women and children who were auctioned there. How nice it would have been to have stood there one hundred and fifty years ago with enough money to purchase every one, and then to say to each, "You are free." This is what Christ has done for us all. Down to the slave markets of sin He went and set us free. The table and its emblems remind us of the awful price He paid.

What begins as a memorial becomes a presence! It is as if one stood before the Washington Monument and suddenly the father of our country is at your side. It is as if you stood in the Lincoln Memorial and suddenly heard a deep voice intoning, "Fourscore and seven years ago." We come here to a memorial to the dying Christ and find ourselves suddenly confronted with the living Christ. Let us go to meet Him, now.

Sermons are not always eloquent, but the Supper never fails to speak peace to our souls. Prayers may not be thoughtful, but this time of meditation brings us close to God. The songs may be ill chosen, but the emblems praise Him still. No person who knows the meaning of the Lord's Supper can ever go away from the place of worship feeling that the hour has been wasted.

In World War I, in a British section of the Western Front, just

14

a few miles back from the front lines, was a hut named Talbot House. It was a meeting place for men going up to the trenches and men coming back. In the loft above they served Communion—truly an upper room and literally a last supper for many men. Over the door were these words: "Abandon rank all ye who enter here." Always, those words are above the place where the table is spread. We are all on the same level here. All of us are sinners—confessing our sins and seeking forgiveness in the only place it can be found—at the foot of the cross. *"The ground is level at the foot of the cross"*

✗ The fires burned brightly at Smithfield—the fires that took the lives of Christian martyrs. On the road from Smithfield a traveler was surprised to see a boy going home. "Where have you been?" he asked. "To Smithfield to see the martyrs burned." "Why on earth would you go there?" "TO LEARN HOW TO DIE," he replied. At the cross we learn how to die—courageously, unselfishly, with forgiveness, praying. AND MORE IMPORTANTLY, at the cross we learn how to live! That's why this Communion Table is so important. It brings us closer to the cross, where Christ teaches us how to die—and how to live!

"But we see Jesus..." begins a text in Hebrews. There are so many places we see Jesus. We see Him in the sunset and we see Him in the shower.

"In the morning I see His face,
In the evening His form I trace,
In the darkness His voice I know:
I see Jesus everywhere I go."

But nowhere do we see Him so clearly as here. The loaf and cup recall His body and His blood. The cross testifies to His love. In the light of that cross we see our sins and seek His forgiveness. Yes, here, above all the other places, "we see Jesus."

The Egyptian cross differs from the familiar one. At the top of the cross is a loop like a handle. Thus, the cross is shaped like the Egyptian hieroglyphic symbol for "life." To the early Christians in Egypt it was an appropriate symbol, for the cross of Christ is, indeed, the Tree of Life.

The Communion begins as a memorial, but it becomes a presence. We are to think of it not so much in terms of marble and stone, not so much in terms of spires and statutes, as in terms of reunion, of fellowship, of family, of rendezvous. Here we honor the dying Christ. Here we meet the living Christ.

The warden of Sing-Sing prison once said that, on the average, an inmate was forgotten by the outside in five years. Friends first ceased to write, then brother and sister, then sweethearts, and mother last of all. But we are never forgotten by God. Of this the Supper reminds us, reassuring us that even when we forget Him, He does not forget us. Though we fail Him, He will not fail us. Even if we forsake Him, He will not forsake us. The limitless, persevering, determined love of God is written here. "For God so loved the world that He gave His only begotten Son."

The Parthenon, that most famous Greek temple, had no secret place, no inner holy room—but was open to all. The Lord's Table is like that. It is a Holy Place, but it is no secret place. All may come here; none are barred save those who come irreverently. Christ invites all Christians, saying, "Whosoever will let him come." We will bar none whom Christ has invited. Let us accept His invitation now.

It took thirteen years to build the famed Brooklyn Bridge that spans the East River. That wider gulf between man and God, Christ bridged in six hours. Three hours under the burning sun and three hours in the eerie darkness, in the midnight at noonday. Six hours of agony—and Christ bridged the gap sin had cut between man and his Maker. Surely, we can take six minutes NOW to meditate upon His sacrificial death.

Soldiers broke down the door of a home where persecuted Christians met in secret; and as they arrested them, they counted the number. "Eleven," said the officer. "Twelve," said the host. The officer counted again. "There are only eleven," he said. "Where is the twelfth?" "Christ," said the Christian. "Christ is here, also." He promised to be here, with us, whenever and wherever this Table is spread. We do not just come here to meet one another. We come to meet Him.

In commenting on the story of the rich man and Lazarus, someone remarked that there is always a great gulf between the cloth and the crumbs. If God had given us only the crumbs from this table of memory, it would have been more than we deserve; but He invites us to sit about it as His guests. In view of such love, we can no longer offer Him the unwanted remnants of our lives, those left over bits of time and treasure that we do not wish to keep. We must, instead, echo the theme of an old hymn:

> All for Jesus, all for Jesus,
> All my being's ransomed powers.
> All my thoughts and words and doings,
> All my days and all my hours.

The Colossus of Rhodes was perhaps the largest monument that ever existed. It towered so high that ships passing into or out of the harbor passed between the gigantic legs of the statue. Indeed, the ancients have described it as so huge a monument that some doubt that it ever existed at all.

But none can doubt that in an upper room long ago Jesus created His own memorial and raised His own monument. We can add no lustre to the fact that this monument is the Lord's Supper. But we can come about it to pay our homage, to see our sins and sorrow for them, and to find forgiveness in His blood. These we do about this table.

The Trojan War was over and Ulyssses was on his way home, about to leave the enchanted island where Calypso lived. She came down to the beach where the ships were putting out to sea and said, "Say good-bye to me but not to the thought of me."

At the cross, men said good-bye to Christ—but not to the thought of Him. And on the very first occasion that they met in memory about this table, CHRIST APPEARED IN THE MIDST. Though our eyes cannot see Him, He is with us now.

PREACHING
RESOURCES

SERMON SERIES

LEADING UP TO RESURRECTION DAY

Cross Ways

It would be possible to develop a very nice series of sermons based on the various shapes of the cross. There is the Anchor Cross (Heb. 6:10); the Budded Cross with trefoil ends that represent the Trinity. You will often see this cross at the top of the staff for the Christian flag. Also the Trinity Cross, which has three fleurs-de-lis and equal arms, stands for the Godhead. The Iona Cross and the Celtic Cross both have a circle superimposed on the cross to signify eternity. There is a graded Latin Cross with a three step base to symbolize Faith, Hope, and Love. The Jerusalem Cross has four smaller crosses in the four corners and suggests the five wounds of Christ. This was the cross carried by the Crusaders. The Egyptian Cross has a loop or handle at the top; thus it is just like the Egyptian hieroglyphic for life. The Russian Cross or Eastern Orthodox Cross has a second horizontal bar near the bottom, which is slanted. Some say this represents the agony of Christ; some say it means his legs were of unequal length. Finally, there is the Cross of Victory, which is a Latin Cross on top of a globe.

If you print your own bulletin covers, then one could be designed for each Sunday displaying the cross that is the inspiration for that sermon. Posters could be made with all the crosses, and then one large one for each of the crosses, displaying it twice—the Sunday before and the Sunday it is used.

ANCHOR

BUDDED

CELTIC

EGYPTIAN GRADED IONA JERUSALEM

TRINITY EASTERN ORTHODOX VICTORY

Self-Portraits of Jesus

This sermon series could center on the "I Am's" of Jesus.

A Long Journey's End — I Am the Way, Truth, and Life

Hope for the Hungry Heart — I Am the Bread of Life

Help for the Helpless — I Am the Good Shepherd

This Is the Life — I Am the Vine

Lord of Life and Death — I Am the Resurrection and the Life

The Seven Words of Men

In 1963, Abingdon Press published a book by Paul L. Moore on the *Seven Words of Men Around the Cross*. A good series can be developed based on these concepts:

The Word of the Passerby — Aha!

The Word of the Soldiers — Let Us Cast Lots

The Word of the Bystanders — Wait

The Word of the High Priests — Come Down

The Word of the Centurion — Truly A Son of God

The Word of the Revolutionary — Remember Me

The Word of the Procurator — I Am Innocent

Faces About the Cross

Abingdon Press also published Clovis Chappel's *Faces About the Cross*. Earlier, Harper published Poteat's *These Shared His Cross*. A series of studies of the individuals who found themselves present at the cross is always appealing: the soldiers, Simon of Cyrene, the women who wept by the way, the thieves, Mary and her friends, John, the disciples watching from afar, Nicodemus, Joseph of Arimathea, the centurion.

The Trees of Life

This series focuses on the various kinds of trees that are mentioned in the gospels during the last week of Christ's ministry.

The Fig Tree — A Living Parable
   (Mark 11:12-14, 20-22, and Matthew 21:18-22)
The Palm Tree — A Loving Tribute
   (John 12:12-18)
The Olive Tree — A Silent Witness
   (Luke 22:39-46)
The Thorn Tree — A Touching Symbol
   (John 19:2-5)
The Evergreen Tree — A Prophetic Emblem
   (Luke 23:31)

Encounters with Jesus

A series could center around those moments when Jesus taught a person one-to-one. It might include the following sermons:

Jesus and the Teacher (Nicodemus)
Jesus and the Fallen Woman (Woman at the Well)
Jesus and the Dishonest Businessman (Zaccheus)
Jesus and the Power Brokers (Caiaphas, Herod, and Pilate)
On Resurrection Day, you could conclude with:
Jesus and the Grieved Friend (Mary Magdalene)

SERMON SERIES
FOR AFTER RESURRECTION DAY

Meeting the Risen Jesus
A series based on five of the resurrection appearances
In the Garden — John 20:11-18
Along the Way — Matthew 28:9, 10
Broken Bread and Opened Eyes — Luke 24:13-35
The Christ of Peace — John 20:19-25
Breakfast by the Sea — John 21:1-25

Relationships of the Resurrection
All too often, the resurrection is seen in a one dimensional view: only in its relationship to our own death. Here is a series showing that the resurrection impacts upon life at more than one place.
The Resurrection and the Judgement of God
   Acts 17:31
The Resurrection and the Operation of God
   Colossians 2:12
The Resurrection and the Godly Life
   Colossians 3:1
The Resurrection and Eternal Life with God
   1 Corinthians 15:12-20

SERMON POSSIBILITIES

The following thoughts are ideas that might easily be developed into sermons. Some, like the first, have obvious major points. Some provide little more than a proposition. Each, however, is the seed for a powerful sermon for emphasizing Christ's resurrection.

The resurrection was validated by the *Open Tomb,* ready for inspection by all; the *Open Mouth* of the disciples, who had formerly been afraid; and the *Open Heart* of the church, ready to accept all men. J.W. Hamilton said: "The empty grave in Palestine is the open mouth of God calling to all the centuries: 'Know you not that you can never defeat the eternal purpose?' "

⊁ The women who came to the tomb had not forgotten the way, had not forgotten their companions, had not forgotten the spices. There was only one thing they had forgotten. They had forgotten Jesus' words!

Quiet power! That's what you see in the resurrection. His rebirth was like His birth. "How silently, how silently, the wondrous gift is given!"

⁕ In the resurrection moment, when the keepers of the tomb became unconscious, living men became as dead men and a dead man came alive!

⊁ The man who had no place to lay His head in life almost had no place to lay His head in death. He was laid to rest, thanks to the generosity of the wealthy Joseph of Arimathea. Even His tomb was borrowed, but that was all right. He only needed it for a short while.

What deserves to be called an earth-shaking event? Certainly, Jesus' death and resurrection qualify. There were literal earthquakes at Golgotha when He died and at the tomb when He arose. The after-shocks can still be felt. Oh, the ground does not literally move when Christ confronts us; but many a soul has been shaken by the crucified and risen One.

Can a person have fear and joy at the same time? It seems that it would be an impossible combination. The women who found the empty tomb felt that way, according to Matthew 28:8. For those who continue to believe in Him, the fear departs but the joy remains.

Don't you think they were embarrassed? The women who discovered Jesus was alive met Him with burial spices in their hands. When we meet Jesus, we are often carrying around symbols of our own lack of faith and insight.

SERMON OUTLINES

THE MORNING AFTER
Mark 16:1-7

The term "morning after" has a very unpleasant connotation, but think of the morning after the resurrection!

I. THE MORNING LIGHT, v. 2
   A. God began Creation with light.
   B. In nature life depends on light.
   C. John said Jesus was the light of men. John 1:4
   D. Jesus said He was the light of the world. John 8:12
   E. Sin is darkness.
   F. Heaven is brightness.
   G. How appropriate—the resurrection at dawn!

II. THE MORNING NEWS, v. 7
   A. Once Jesus said, "Tell no man." Luke 8:56
   B. Now He says, "Go and tell!"
   C. At first they hesitated, then responded eagerly.
      Mark 16:10; Matthew 28:8; Luke 24:33-35; Acts 8:4
   D. We, too, must go and tell eagerly. Acts 1:8; Luke 24:46-48; Matthew 28:19; Mark 16:15

III. THE MORNING GLORY, v. 5
   A. Moses' face shone with God's glory. Exodus 34:29
   B. The temple was filled with a cloud of glory.
      I Kings 8:10
   C. Jesus was transfigured gloriously. Luke 9:29
   D. None compared to the radiance from the empty tomb.
   E. None compared to the glory of the risen Christ.
   F. Such a glory awaits us. 2 Corinthians 4:17; Revelation 21:23

We are children of the dawn. Let us walk in the light.

THE LAST THINGS
1 Corinthians 15:51-58

People are keenly interested in the last words of famous men, the last works of famous writers, painters, and musicians, and in the last things of our religion.

I. THE LAST MYSTERY, v. 51

   A. Birth is a mystery.

   B. Life is a mystery.

   C. Death is a mystery.

   D. Life after death is the last mystery.

II. THE LAST TRUMPET, v. 52

   A. The certainty of it

   B. The finality of it

   C. The result of it

III. THE LAST ENEMY, vs. 55-57 and 15:25, 26

   A. We don't win the victory ourselves.

   B. God gives the victory.

   C. God gives it through Christ.

   D. We reflect it in life. Colossians 3:1; Romans 6:2-4

What a blessed assurance that Jesus is risen, that we, too, shall rise, and that our labor for Him is not in vain.

4-1987

GIFTS FROM THE RISEN CHRIST
John 20:19-23

INTRODUCTION:
Paul said that when Jesus "led captivity captive," he gave gifts unto men. We may see those gifts here in the upper room.

I. HE BROUGHT PEACE FOR THEIR HEARTS, v. 19
   A. From the turmoil of fear
   B. From the tyranny of doubt
   C. From the terror of loneliness

II. HE BROUGHT PROOF FOR THEIR MINDS, v. 20
   A. The Risen One is the Crucified One
   B. Surprising One is the Familiar One

III. HE BROUGHT PURPOSE FOR THEIR LIVES
   A. They shared His purpose, v. 21
   B. They ministered His grace, v. 23

IV. HE BROUGHT POWER FOR THEIR SERVICE, v. 22
   A. It was more than the power of a great intellect.
   B. It was more than the power of a determined heart.
   C. It was more than the power of complete dedication.
   D. It was more than the power of wealth or arms.
   E. It was the power of the Holy Spirit of God.

V   pg 61   He brought
His Personal Presence

CONCLUSION:
The risen Christ would give these gifts to all His followers, but first they must (like the early disciples) wait and watch and pray.

LOOK
Matthew 28:1-8

The amazing appearance of the angels at the tomb gave the women something to think about. They were compelled to look at three things.

I. LOOK AT YOURSELVES, vs. 5, 6

    A.   This is not a time for fear.

    B.   This is not a time for surprise.

II. LOOK AT THE FACTS, v. 6

    A.   Christianity is a faith based on fact.

    B.   Christianity is a faith that invites examination.

III. LOOK TOWARD THE FUTURE, v. 7

    A.   Hope is ahead.

    B.   Work is ahead.

    C.   Christ is ahead.

The church has the promise, in the light of the resurrection, that Jesus goes ahead of us wherever we must go.

RESURRECTION AND RESTORATION
John 21:15-19

Peter knew the Lord was risen but did not know the Lord still had a ministry for him. When the risen Lord talked to Peter by the sea, He emphasized that Peter could be restored to a place of usefulness.

I. PETER WAS CALLED TO A MINISTRY OF LOVE, vs. 15-17

   A. Love is a test of commitment.

   B. Love is the motive of ministry.

II. PETER WAS CALLED TO A MINISTRY OF SERVICE, vs. 15-17

   A. Feed the flock.

   B. Protect the flock.

   C. Guide the flock.

III. PETER WAS CALLED TO A MINISTRY OF SACRIFICE, vs. 18, 19

   A. Duty glorifies God.

   B. Death glorifies God.

   C. Discipleship glorifies God.

Though there were times when Peter had let his Lord down, ultimately he fulfilled his ministry. He was able to be restored because Christ was risen.

LIFE BEYOND DEATH
Job 14:14

The question we see in our text is the oldest question of man. In examining Job's confrontation with this question in Chapter 14, what do we learn of life after death?

I. MAN DESIRES IT

    A.   Because life is difficult, vs. 1, 2

    B.   Because life is short, vs. 1, 2

    C.   Because he longs to be with God, vs. 13, 14

II. NATURE SUGGESTS IT

    A.   The tree is reproduced. vs. 7-10

    B.   The water is recycled. vs. 11, 12

    C.   The man ought to be resurrected.

III. LOVE DEMANDS IT

    A.   The love that created us, v. 15

    B.   The love that called us, v. 15

    C.   The love that converted us, vs. 16, 17

The conclusion of the matter is found in Job 19:25-27 when Job confidently affirms, "I will see him."

THE WRONG SIDE OF "EASTER"
Matthew 28:1-15

INTRODUCTION:
- A. James S. Stewart says we are living on the wrong side of "Easter."

- B. We have fifty-two "Easters" every year—we are a creation of "Easter."

I. WE NEED LESS MOURNING AND MORE CELEBRATION

- A. Our leader lives.

- B. Our cause is true.

- C. We shall live, also.

II. WE NEED LESS FEAR AND MORE CONFIDENCE

- A. Can sin harm us?

- B. Is there more to life?

- C. Can death harm us?

III. WE NEED LESS APATHY AND MORE COMMITMENT

- A. This truth is the best news in the world.

- B. This truth is essential.

- C. This truth must be told to all.

CONCLUSION:
We are facing the most unbelievable, yet most important, fact of history.

THE GLORIOUS EXCHANGE
1 Corinthians 15:50-57

When Christ rose from the dead as the firstfruit of many others, He allowed us to exchange uncertainties for certainties.

    I. WHEN, NOT IF. vs. 50-52
       A. The certainty of death
       B. The certainty of the day of the Lord

    II. MUST, NOT MIGHT. v. 53
       A. Job had this confidence (Job 19:25-27)
       B. Jesus had this confidence (John 16:16, 17, 28, 29)
       C. Paul had this confidence (2 Corinthians 5:1)

    III. ETERNAL, NOT MORTAL. v. 53
       A. We are more than flesh and blood
       B. We are meant for heaven — not earth
       C. We are made for eternity — not time

    IV. LIFE, NOT DEATH. vs. 54-57
       A. Life transforms death
       B. Life transcends death
       C. Life triumphs over death

    V. VICTORY, NOT DEFEAT. vs. 54-57
       A. Christ won the victory for us
       B. The Father gives the victory to us

Who would not want to make this exchange? Everyone has that opportunity. All can exchange defeat for victory.

THE MYSTERY OF THE CROSS
Luke 18:31-34

This is a comforting text. It consoles us to know that the disciples, like us, did not always understand. We are reassured that we don't have to understand everything to be a disciple.

I. HOW CAN THE KINGDOM BE ADVANCED BY A CROSS?
   A. It is contrary to common sense.
   B. It is contrary to history.
   C. It is contrary to our experience.
   D. It is compatible with prophecy.
   E. It is compatible with the nature of Christ.

II. HOW CAN MEN BE SO CRUEL TO CHRIST?
   A. He deserves a medal, not mocking.
   B. It shows how far evil will go.
   C. It shows how much love will endure.

III. HOW CAN A GOOD MAN SUFFER?
   A. The question is as old as the book of Job.
   B. The question is as fresh as your present pain.
   C. The experience of Christ reassures us.
   D. The experience of Christ comforts us.
   E. The experience of Christ strengthens us.

IV. HOW CAN DEATH BE OVERCOME?
   A. Human observation argues against it.
   B. Human intuition argues for it.
   C. Christ's resurrection settles it.

Often we believe what we cannot understand. It is not understanding that saves us. It is faith.

THE CHRIST OF THE RESURRECTION
Luke 24:13-32

There is always the danger that our preoccupation with the day may distract us from the Divine Christ in whose honor the day is kept.

I. THE INESCAPABLE CHRIST, vs. 15, 16

   A. The sealed door of the tomb could not keep Him in.

   B. The locked door of the Upper Room could not keep Him out.

   C. He still breaks through barriers to come to us.

   D. He is still the Unrecognized Presence.

II. THE INDISPENSABLE CHRIST, vs. 21-26

   A. In Him alone we have hope.

   B. He alone fulfills prophecy.

   C. He alone gives assurance of life hereafter.

III. THE INCENDIARY CHRIST, v. 32

   A. He lights the fires of faith. John 20:30, 31

   B. He rekindles the fires of commitment.

   C. He fans the flames of service.

Christ is never very far from us; but we must let Him into our lives. He will never force himself upon us.

THE INEVITABILITY OF THE RESURRECTION
Acts 2:24

INTRODUCTION:
The Bible names many impossible things (Hebrews 6:18; 11:6). The most touching impossibility is here: that Christ should be conquered by death. The resurrection was inevitable.

I. IT WAS INEVITABLE BECAUSE OF WHAT JESUS SAID
   A. John 2:19
   B. Matthew 16:21
   C. Matthew 17:22, 23
   D. Mark 14:27, 28

II. IT WAS INEVITABLE BECAUSE OF WHO JESUS WAS
   A. Acts 2:33-36
   B. In Him was life. John 1:4
   C. He was the resurrection. John 11:25
   D. He was before Abraham. John 8:58
   E. Psalm 16:8-11

III. IT WAS INEVITABLE BECAUSE GOD WAS WITH HIM
   A. Acts 2:22
   B. John 5:17-30
   C. John 10:15-18

IV. IT WAS INEVITABLE BECAUSE OF THE CONSEQUENCES IF HE HAD NOT
   A. The universe would disintegrate. Colossians 1:17
   B. There would be no future. 1 Corinthians 15:12-19
   C. There would be no forgiveness. 1 Corinthians 15:17
   D. There would be no faith. 1 Corinthians 15:14-17

CONCLUSION:
We have seen the consequences if Christ had not risen. What are the consequences now that He has risen?

THE RAISING OF THE REJECTED STONE
Matthew 21:42-46 with Psalm 119:22

INTRODUCTION:
When the New Testament quotes the Old, we must pay attention. In this text, it is Jesus himself who is quoting. Again, we must pay attention.

I. MAN'S REJECTION

A. Prophesied beforehand

B. Even now in preparation, v. 46

C. Eventually carried out

D. Everlastingly punished, v. 43, 44

II. GOD'S RESURRECTION

A. God is wiser than man.

B. God is more powerful than death.

C. God is too loving not to intervene.

D. God always announces in advance His mightiest acts.

III. OUR RESPONSE

A. It is marvelous in our eyes.

B. We must do more than marvel; we must believe.

C. We must do more than believe; we must worship.

D. We must do more than worship; we must serve.

CONCLUSION:
We marvel at God's power. We marvel at His love. We marvel at His grace.

THE CARPENTER'S TEMPLE
John 2:18-22

INTRODUCTION:

Bible students say there were three temples in Jerusalem: one built by Solomon, one by Ezra, and one by Nehemiah. There was a fourth. It was built by a carpenter from Nazareth named Jesus.

I. THE CENTER OF OUR RELIGION, v. 21
   A. It is Christ.
   B. It is not a nation, Israel.
   C. It is not a place, Jerusalem.
   D. It is not a building, the temple.
   E. We still face the temptation to limit our religion to certain nations, places, and buildings.

II. THE CERTAINTY OF OUR RELIGION, v. 19
   A. It is based on the resurrection of Jesus.
   B. It is based on fulfilled predictions Jesus made.
   C. It is fact, not fiction.
   D. It is objective, not subjective.

III. THE CELEBRATION OF OUR RELIGION, v. 22
   A. It is a celebration of remembrance.
   B. It is a celebration of faith.
   C. It is a celebration of Scripture.
   D. It is a personal fellowship with a present and living Lord.

CONCLUSION:

It is a mark of the maturity of man that we no longer need visible symbols: temples and lambs and altars of incense. It is a mark of God's trust in us that He offers us now an invisible Christ, a walk by faith, and a truly spiritual religion.

✝ **A DREAM COME TRUE**
John 20:1-9, 19, 20

Peter received a knock on the door, and heard news that changed his life. The news was the answer to all his hopes. Did Jesus really rise?

I. HE WAS COMPELLED BY THE POSSIBILITY, vs. 2-4

    A. Job suggested it. Job 14:14

    B. David believed it. Psalm 16:9, 10

    C. Jesus promised it. Matthew 16:21

    D. The heart desires it.

II. HE WAS CONFRONTED WITH THE EVIDENCE, vs. 5-9

    A. The evidence of what was there

    B. The evidence of what was not there

    C. The testimony of the women

    D. The testimony of Scripture

III. HE WAS CONVINCED BY THE PRESENCE OF THE LORD, vs. 19, 20

    A. His doubt was replaced by faith.

    B. His fear was replaced by courage.

    C. His sadness was replaced by joy.

The proof of the resurrection is not just the empty tomb; it is the living Lord.

FACING THE DAWN
Luke 24:13-35

INTRODUCTION:

Going from Jerusalem to Emmaus, the disciples were literally heading west, literally facing the sunset. After their encounter with Christ, they turned around and went back to Jerusalem, facing east, facing the dawn.

Until Christ rose from the dead, all humanity faced west, faced the sunset. Now, like them, we may turn about and face east, facing the dawn.

I. IT MEANT THE DAWNING OF A NEW DAY.

    A. Literally, it was a new day. Was it by chance that He arose in the morning? Perhaps, and yet the poet in us finds it fitting.

    B. For the disciples, it was a new day.

        1. They go from hiding behind closed doors to striding across the world with the gospel.

        2. They go from huddling together in despair to scattering everywhere in joyous evangelism.

        3. They go from weeping over a lost cause to shouting over a wonderful victory!

    C. For us, it was a new day.

        1. The resurrection bespeaks continuing victories.

        2. As some flowers grow best when placed to get the morning sun, so churches grow best when facing the dawn!

        3. The world's misery, gloom, and despair give way to new hope and joy. *(continued)*

41

II. IT MEANT THE LEARNING OF A NEW LESSON.

A. God's plan included redemptive suffering.

B. God's plan can never be thwarted.

C. God's plan is advanced by the very things that seem to defeat it.

D. Our lives are a part of God's plan.

III. IT MEANT THE CONFIRMING OF AN OLD HOPE.

A. It is mankind's oldest hope.

B. It is mankind's most universal hope. You read about it in the Psalms and the book of Job, in Plato and in Socrates, in Tennyson and Churchill.

C. Without the resurrection, it is mankind's most fragile hope.

D. With the resurrection, it is mankind's most virile hope.

CONCLUSION:
Now the mournful voices of despair can—no—*must* give way to the triumphant voices of victory: Victory in Jesus!

HE IS HERE
Matthew 28:6

INTRODUCTION:

We like to take texts and reset them in our own time and place. So when God says, "I have loved you with an everlasting love," we think of ourselves. When Jesus looks into the eyes of Peter and says, "Do you love me?" He seems to look into our eyes as well.

This is a very good thing to do with a text; but it will not work with this text: "He is not here!" For He is here! Matthew 28:6 can never be translated into our day because Matthew 28:20 turns it around!

I. THE NEGATIVE IS TURNED TO A POSITIVE.

    A. You can't build your life on negatives.

    B. The fact that the tomb was empty is only half of the story.

    C. It is not just the empty tomb, but the filled hearts of men that spell victory.

II. THE END IS TURNED INTO A BEGINNING.

    A. Pilate and the chief priests thought they had written a conclusion to the story of Christ when, in fact, they had only written an introduction.

    B. The pagan world hunted out the Christians and thought their persecution would end world evangelism. It only accelerated it.

    C. The conclusion to the story of Christ can never be written, for it has no conclusion.

    D. If your life is entwined with Christ's, your life will never have a conclusion! *(continued)*

III. THE DARKNESS IS TURNED INTO LIGHT.

A. The darkness of the tomb gives way to the brilliance of His appearing.

B. The darkness of night gives way to the brightness of dawning.

C. The darkness of sin gives way to the beauty of forgiveness.

D. The darkness of despair gives way to the glory of hope.

CONCLUSION:
Emptiness is turned into fulness. As long as the tomb is filled, hearts and hopes are empty. When the tomb is empty, then hearts and hopes are filled.

THE WORLD'S MOST FUTILE EFFORT
or
MAKE IT AS SECURE AS YOU CAN
Matthew 27:65 (R.S.V.)

INTRODUCTION:
Why Pilate's choice of words? Does he half believe that they couldn't make it secure?

I. MAKING THE TOMB SECURE
    A. It was impossible when the tomb held the body of the Lord of life. (Acts 2:24)
    B. It was impossible so long as God was on His throne.
    C. It was impossible so long as there was justice in the universe.

II. MAKING YOUR LIFE SECURE
    A. It is not possible to do it with money.
    B. It is not possible to do it with health.
    C. It is not possible to do it with fame.
    D. It is not possible to do it with family.
    E. It is not possible to do it with armed guards.
    F. It is only possible with Christ.

III. MAKING YOUR FUTURE SECURE
    A. Future means more than life here on earth.
    B. Future means more than death. It refers to that which lies beyond death.
    C. Without Christ there is no certainty regarding eternity.
    D. With Christ there is complete certainty regarding eternity.

CONCLUSION:
It is futile to try to make your life or your future secure by yourself. Even if you make it as secure as you can, it is not safe. The only security is in the victorious, resurrected Christ!

ILLUSTRATIONS

The later years of life are often called the Sunset years; but they are, in fact, the Sunrise years. Since Jesus rose from the dead, life faces east, not west. "Beyond the Sunset" is a beautiful hymn; but we really ought to speak of beyond the sunrise. Peter said we lived our lives "until the day dawn and the day-star arise in your hearts" (2 Peter 1:19).

Dr. Pedro Ara Sarria perfected a technique for preserving the body and applied it to Argentina's Eva Peron. The embalmed body was kept intact but, for political reasons, was moved from place to place. It went from his laboratory in Buenos Aries to a military camp, to a dusty storeroom in Bonn, Germany, to a secret grave in Milan, Italy, to an attic in Madrid, back to a chapel in Argentina, and finally to a family tomb. What happens to our bodies after we die may not be very important. What happens to the spirit, the true person, is very important. Whether our bodies are buried, cremated, lost in an explosion, or buried at sea, it makes no difference. The real concern is that the soul be at home with God.

It was Joseph Cook who said, "Pillow my head on no guesses when I die." Paul spoke of our future in the strongest possible terms. In 2 Corinthians 5:1ff he says, "We *know*." He doesn't say, "We think, we hope, we believe, we trust, we expect" but "we *know*." Guesses are little comfort. We want assurance, blessed assurance.

✱ Matineua said, "We do not believe in immortality because we can not prove it, but we try to prove it because we cannot help believing in it." Emerson said, "When God wants to carry a point with his children, He plants His arguments into the instincts." Certainly, we have an instinct for immortality, an affinity for the infinite. We feel certain there is more beyond this life. If there is not, then our own nature has played on us a cruel joke. The risen Christ assures us that our instincts are right.

We wonder about the life of the man whose epitaph read,
    Don't bother me now
    Don't bother me never
    I want to be dead
    For ever and ever.
Most of us have not found that life is bad; and most of us want
to live for ever and ever. Through Christ, we are assured that
we can do just that.
    I heard the voice of Jesus say
    I am this dark world's light
    Look unto me thy morn shall rise
    And all thy day be bright.

Robert MacNeil wrote, "I associate different emotions with
traveling toward the different points of the compass. Going
east is going back to where we all came from, toward the
dawn; to the west is escape, adventure, the pull of the sunset.
Going south brings an anticipation of languor, of being
enfolded in limpid air. But when I head north, my blood
quickens—it takes a special people to live where nature makes
it so hard." Spiritually, we can all agree that going east is going
where all came from. Our spiritual fountainhead is Easter
Sunday, our spiritual source is the resurrection of Jesus. All of
the Christian religion flows from this single place.

Good Friday and the Saturday before Easter are very special
days in Greece. In every church, there is a flower-bedecked
picture to represent the bier of Christ. Four soldiers stand
guard on either corner throughout the night and day, from
Good Friday until Easter Sunday. The visitor often wonders if
they are there in a re-enactment of the soldiers guarding the
tomb of Jesus. If so, it would be exciting to see them faint as the
real soldiers did at the resurrection. One suspects, however,
that it is rather an honor guard. If so, it is a very nice symbol.
Whatever our symbols, dreams, and ceremonies, all of us
agree that the best honor one may pay to Christ is to believe in
Him and to live for Him. Easter is more than a celebration. It
makes its demands upon us.

The late Queen Wilhelmina of the Netherlands was a pious
Christian, as was her husband Hendrik. They had discussed

death. Since both regarded it as the start of a new life, they had promised each other that their funerals would not be shrouded in black, but rather be completely white as a symbol of light. Even the dress the Queen wore to Hendrik's funeral was white. It is true that for the Christian, death is not darkness but light, not black with despair, but bright with hope.

On Good Friday evening, each Greek Orthodox church has a service. Afterward, the holy picture that represents Christ, decorated with flowers and candles, is brought to the village square. A solemn procession comes from each church; and a brief service is held. Then, on Saturday night, a second service is held. Just before midnight, the church is plunged into darkness. Suddenly, one lighted candle appears in the sanctuary. The worshipers light their own candles from it and pass on the fire to others. Bells ring. Fireworks greet the resurrection. Each person carries his light home. (Ought we all not carry the light of the resurrection and the gospel into our daily lives?) Then, on Sunday morning, another procession retraces the steps of the previous Friday night. This time, it is no flower-covered coffin, but a picture of the risen Lord that is carried. The music is joyful and triumphant. Christ is alive forevermore! The parallels are obvious. With a dead Christ, we are sad; and we live our lives in darkness. With a risen Christ, we are joyful; and we live our lives in the light. It is a light that cannot be kept at church but must be carried home. It is a light that cannot be selfishly hoarded but must be shared with others.

On Good Friday in Athens, the street lights are turned off, some public buildings are draped in black, and a slow-moving procession winds through the streets. At midnight, on Easter Eve, a cannon booms from the top of Mt. Lycabettus, which towers above the city. Thousands worshiping at the church of St. George on the summit light their candles. Slowly they pass down the twisting path from the summit to the city below. One can see thousands of tiny pin points of light moving down the mountain and into the city. So the truth of Easter must come down from the mountain of spiritual worship and walk the streets of daily need.

Among the people from Eastern Europe, the Easter basket

had nothing to do with candy and rabbits. Baskets were filled with symbolic things and taken to church to be blessed. There was bread in the basket to recall how Israel relied on God in the wilderness and to symbolize life. Horseradish was there to suggest the bitterness of Egyptian bondage and the bitterness of Jesus' death. Salt was there as a symbol of our common humanity. Ham was there as a reminder that we are not under the old law, which forbade so much, but under the new. Eggs were in the basket, too. They stood for hope and resurrection and life! Whatever our customs, whatever our symbols, Easter always stands for new life, for resurrection, for hope!

Blandon Churchyard, where Winston Churchill is buried, is like many similar village churchyards. There is a lych-gate at the entrance. Here the bearers could wait with the casket until the minister came out to escort them into the church. If the weather were inclement, they had some shelter beneath the roof of the lych-gate. Over the lych-gate at Blandon are these words, "I know that my Redeemer liveth." One sees them, not upon entering, but upon leaving! How comforting to a family who has just left the body of a loved one in the churchyard! How comforting it is to us all to remember we have a deathless Redeemer!

A man said that one year he had two Easters. After the Easter celebration in America, he went to Greece. In the Orthodox Church, Easter usually comes a week later than the Catholic and Protestant Easter. So he enjoyed two Easter Sundays. We were meant to enjoy fifty-two Easter Sundays! Every Sunday, every first day of the week, commemorates the resurrection of Jesus from the dead. It is not just one day a year. That would not be enough. It is one day in every week! That's how important the resurrection is!

There are many stories, sagas, and legends that have in them the theme of death and resurrection. That ought not to surprise us nor disturb us. Anything genuine is bound to have its counterfeits. In fact, the presence of the counterfeit reassures us of the fact of the genuine.

Who would believe that the caterpillar becomes a butterfly

unless he had seen it. If we can accept that, how can we deny that death can be transformed into life.

The city of Phoenix, Arizona, owes its name to a legendary bird that rose out of the ashes of a funeral pyre. The first explorers in Arizona came upon prehistoric remains of dwellings and canals, so they felt they were building again on the ashes of the past. Our funeral ritual says "ashes to ashes, dust to dust"; yet the resurrection teaches us just the opposite. Burial is not a return to our origins, but merely a transition. We do not go from dust to dust. We go from life to life.

Art galleries in New York and Florida have been exhibiting the paintings of Jacob J. Kass. His work is unique because he never paints on canvas. He paints on saws: hand saws, circular saws, all kinds of saws. He takes old, dull, rusty, worn-out saw blades and paints on them scenes of striking beauty. In a far, far, far larger way, God takes the ugliness of death and paints on it a picture of life.

Two men were arguing about sports. One said that boxing was the most violent of all sports. The other said it was hockey, because in hockey they didn't just go at each other with their fists—they used sticks! The wives were listening and one of them disagreed.

"I think baseball is the most violent sport."

"That's ridiculous," they answered. "Baseball is not a violent sport. Why would you say that?"

"Well," she said, "the other day I overheard an announcer say that in one inning three men died on base."

We may speak of death in a joke, but death is not a joking matter. We may speak of it in a trifling way. We may speak of it in a superficial manner. "I was so embarrassed I could have died"; but death is no superficial or trifling matter. Perhaps we use the word in all these ways to mask our fears. The Bible takes death seriously. It calls it our enemy. The Bible never minimizes death. It maximizes Christ's victory over death.

From all over the world, people come to Florence to see Michelangelo's famous "David," one of the most beautiful and one of the most celebrated statues in the world. Looking at it in the great hall of the University, one finds the story behind it hard to believe; but the story is true. That lovely piece of art was made from a rejected stone. For fifty years it lay in the work yard behind the Duomo at Florence. Duccio had tried to make something of it but gave it up, leaving a great gash in the middle. Only a Michaelangelo could see what possibilities lay in that piece of marble! In a far, far larger way, Christ was the rejected stone, elevated to the most important place, a fulfillment of ancient prophecy!

The largest man-made structure on earth is a tomb, the Great Pyramid. The oldest man-made structure on earth is a tomb, the step pyramid at Sakkara. The only one of the seven wonders of the world that still stands is a tomb—the Pyramids! Thus do we show man's preoccupation with death. Paul speaks of those who all their lifetime were subject to bondage through fear! We see that throughout history, men have feared death most of all. Christianity is not preoccupied with death. It is preoccupied with life!

It was said of the people of Rhodes that "they eat as if they were about to die and build as if they were immortal." There is a sense in which we ought to conduct ourselves as if we were about to die. Not that we indulge ourselves foolishly, but that we make our time on earth count. We ought to live holy and productive lives, as if any day might be our last. But we are, in fact, immortal. We ought, in quite another way, to live as immortal beings. We are going to spend eternity some place. We are determining that now and preparing ourselves for it. The immortality of the soul can be a very comforting doctrine or a very frightening doctrine. Are you living as one about to die? Are you living as one immortal?

When Julius Caesar came to Alexandria, they showed him the coffin of Alexander the Great. They then asked him if he would like to see Ptolemy's coffin. He said, "I came to see a king, not a corpse." When we come to church, we come to see a King, not a corpse!

Do you know the song?
Because He lives, I can face tomorrow;

52

Because He lives, all fear is gone.
Because I know He holds the future;
And life is worth the living just because He lives.
Sometimes the problem is not facing tomorrow. Sometimes it is facing yesterday. The past may trouble as much as the future may make anxious. But because He lives, we can face both the past and the future, both yesterday and tomorrow.

We have so many ways to avoid the word *death*. We say he "went away." We say he "passed away." We say he was "taken." We say he "fell asleep." Far better to face death squarely and call it what it is. The Bible does that and labels death our enemy. Faith gives us the courage to look death in the eye because we know that death for a believer is only a transition. It is never an end.

Recently, newspapers told the story of a woman who was separated from her father at age two. Now, forty-two years later, she is to finally meet him. When she located him, half way across the nation, they talked on the phone for two hours! Now they were planning a grand reunion. The headline for that story read, "42 Year Wait to Meet Father." That's what life is—waiting to meet our Father. We may have to wait eighty or ninety years, but life is only waiting to meet our Father. When you know that, death loses its sting.

It has been said, "At the end of the game, the king and the queen and the pawns all go into the same box." That's true of our bodies but not of our souls. The grave is the lot of us all. Death comes to powerful and ordinary, rich and poor, famous and obscure. But we are more than our bodies; and at the end of the game, we do not really all go into the same box. Some hear the words, "Come, blessed of my Father," and they enter into everlasting life. Others hear the words, "Depart from me; I never knew you," and they enter into everlasting death.

In the huge, new Dallas/Fort Worth airport is the skeleton of a plesiosaur. His bones were found in the building of the airport. The plesiosaur is a great lizard, twenty-five feet long and weighing ten thousand pounds. It is said the plesiosaur lived seventy million years ago. The contrast is striking. Here is one of the most modern airports in the world and in the midst of it a skeleton seventy million years old. We have a similar contrast in the resurrection. The Gospels tell us that the grave in which Jesus was placed was near Golgotha. So the place of His death and the place of His resurrection were side by side. The day of His death and the day of His resurrection were side by side, only one day apart. We who are always close to death may, by faith, also be close to life—life like His, life everlasting!

At a world gathering of religious leaders the spokesman for Christianity came to the heart of the matter when he said, "Religion means to me victory, victory, victory!" That *is* the thrust of our faith. Christianity means victory over sin! Christianity means victory over death! Christianity means victory over the grave! Christianity means victory over Hell itself!

How often in our experience does a death bring about a reconciliation? Sometimes it is a reconciliation in a family. Sometimes it is a reconciliation among friends. Sometimes it is a reconciliation in a congregation. Often, death brings about a reconciliation. Christ's death brings about the most important reconciliation of all. He has reconciled us to God by His death on the cross.

Dying words are often illuminating. When Henry David Thoreau was asked if he had made peace with God, he said, "We never quarreled." Rabelais, the French writer, said, "I am going to seek a great perhaps." Oscar Wilde was calling for champagne and said, "I am dying as I have lived—beyond my means." Max Baer's dying words were: "Oh, God, here I go!"

The cartoon "This Funny World" once showed a couple leaving church. The wife is saying, "I'll tell you why it's always the same old sermon. The only time you come is on Easter Sunday, that's why!"

When the great preacher, William Sangster, was terminally ill with cancer, he was living with his daughter. He could get about but could not speak. One Easter Sunday morning, he seemed especially despondent. Finally he wrote on his pad: "What tragedy! Resurrection Lord's Day and no voice with which to praise my great Redeemer's name." Then he sat dejectedly gazing out the window. Finally, he wrote again: "There is only one thing more tragic—to have a voice and fail to praise the great Redeemer's Name."

The common denominators of all religions is the conviction that this life is not all there is.

When Bishop Brown of the Episcopal Church came to speak in Virginia's historic St. Luke's Church, Isle of Wight county, he said, "It has been said that Bishop Brown wants to be buried in St. Luke's graveyard. That's nonsense. I'm here to tell you that Bishop Brown doesn't want to be buried anywhere."

In "The Romance of the Last Crusade," British Major Vivian Gilbert told of his advance toward Jerusalem during World War I. He stopped one night to visit a field hospital. He stayed by the bedside of a dying soldier, barely nineteen. He told their location. They were at Emmaus. Then he told him the story from Luke of two men on their way to Emmaus and the appearance of the risen Christ to them. He told him how Jesus ate with them that day. "And it happened right here, on this very spot!" he said. A look of peace and comfort told the major that the story had done its work.

"Why is this night different from all other nights?" This is the question which is asked in every Jewish home at Passover. It is always asked by the youngest child; and it offers an opportunity to explain the rescue of Israel from Egypt. So we may ask of the day of Christ's resurrection, why is this day different from all other days? The answer is the most important ever given!

Even if we were not promised Heaven, would death have to be that bad? Would death be too stiff a price to pay for the privilege of living? That is the price. Everything that lives also dies. From the smallest, single-celled organism to the most complex—man, animal, and plant—all things that live also die. If you would prefer to be a rock, you would never die; but you would never live either. How much greater it is, though, to have the confidence that this life is not all there is.

55

The first law of Thermodynamics says that no mass or energy is ever destroyed, that it merely changes form. When a piece of wood is burned, it is not gone. Some of it becomes heat; some deteriorates into the ashes. But it is not destroyed— it just changes. When a lake dries up, the water is gone. It has evaporated into the air, only to fall to earth again someday. If we can see this all around us in the physical world, is it so hard to conceive of it in the spiritual world? Harry Emerson Fosdick said, "Can it be that God is the most unscrupulous waster in the universe—making great personalities, only to throw them utterly away." If we can see it in nature, can we see it in the sphere of faith? We, too, can have the same confidence that the apostle Paul had when he said, "We shall all be changed."

John Wooden, the famous basketball coach, always keeps a cross in his pocket. He says he keeps it there to remind himself that there is something more important in life than basketball! The cross ought to remind us that there is something more important in life than anything else and everything else—that is that Jesus died and rose again. That's more important than politics. That's more important than business. That's more important than romance. That's more important than education. That's more important than your career. That's more important than your health. That's more important than your safety. That's more important than your very life!

The epitaph for one of the first Virginians buried at Jamestown reads, "A Great Sinner Confidently Awaiting A Joyous Resurrection."

We have so beautified the cross that we often forget that it was really a hideous instrument of cruel torture. In the Passion Play at Oberammergau, Germany, the man who plays the part of Christ carries a cross weighing eighty pounds and hangs on it for twenty minutes. We do not know how much the cross of Christ weighed, but He hung on it for six long hours of agony until death came. We make it beautiful because of the way it has blessed us. We make it beautiful because it made our lives beautiful. We make it beautiful because it expresses a beautiful love. The cross is not the only ugly thing made beautiful by Jesus Christ!

In 1917, work was completed on the Quebec Bridge over the St. Lawrence River. At that time, it was the world's longest span. Eighty-six men died to bridge the river. There is a longer span. It bridges the gulf between a sinful man and a holy God. Only one man died to make that bridge possible. We honor Him!

Warren K. Robinson preached that he, himself, was divine. When he became gravely ill, his followers would not allow a blood transfusion. "This is God," they said. "No mere mortal blood could be allowed to enter the veins of God." Warren K. Robinson died because they would not put the blood of men into a "god." But in a sense, the reverse happened at Calvary. Would it be crude to say that on the cross man received a Divine blood transfusion? Isn't that what forgiveness is all about?

Jesus did not liken the kingdom of God to a diamond, but to a pearl. Of all precious stones, the pearl has the humblest origin. It begins with a wound and is created out of God's resources for healing the wound. So the kingdom begins with a wound, the wound in the body of Jesus. Then we marvel at God's resources for healing: physically, mentally, spiritually!

A legend says an emperor found a nail from the cross. With it he made a bit for his horse's bridle. When he rode into battle after that, he always overcame his enemies because of that piece of iron. Ah, the cross is not there to be used by us to our advantage. The cross is there so that we may be used by God to His advantage!

A few years ago, a French court refused to rule on whether the Jews or the Romans were responsible for the death of Jesus. The occasion was a claim for damages against the author of a book entitled The True Trial of Jesus. The author had been defamed, ruled the court, by a minister who called him a renegade Christian because he put the blame on the Romans. The court awarded damages of one franc! Of course, we already know who is to blame for the death of Jesus. It is not the Jews! It is not the Romans! We, ourselves, are to blame! He died for our sins!

In Savannah, Georgia, there are numerous monuments to Civil War battles and to those who died in them. One bears this inscription from Ezekiel 37:9, "Come from the four winds, O breath, and breathe upon these slain, that they may live." It is beautifully poetic to think of the breath of God that first brought life in Eden coming again to restore life to the dead. However, we understand that life beyond death is really the gift of the risen Christ. It comes only through His power.

A five-year-old girl was very, very fond of her Vacation Bible School teacher. She called her on the phone to talk. "I pray for you every night," she said. "I pray you'll live forever!" That's a sweet prayer. While death is the universal lot of us all, it is also true that Christians live forever. Christ's own resurrection ensures an answer to the child's prayer.

The great majority of art that remains from ancient Egypt, Greece, and Rome is funerary art. It is art that comes from tombs or memorials; art that speaks of death. In the museum at Thessalonica, there is a great collection of gold objects. All are from tombs, from the great garments of death. Christianity draws our attention away from death to life. Not that death can be ignored, or should be ignored. It is rather that we see life, both now and beyond the grave, as the most significant of all concerns. It does no good to ornament death with gold or marble. It is still death and still our enemy. It is better by far to ornament life with good deeds and to spend our money, time, and art on those things that make life more abundant, more lasting, and more blessed.

King Baldwin I was crowned king of Jerusalem *in Bethlehem* because he refused to be crowned with a gold crown in the city where the Lord was crowned with a crown of thorns.
>King of my life, I crown Thee now,
>Thine shall the glory be!
>Lest I forget thy thorn-crowned brow,
>Lead me to Calvary!

In the Canadian province of Quebec, there is a custom that is observed every January third. It dates from the fifth century. It consists of the baking, blessing, and giving away of little loaves of bread. Every year they give away fifty thousand of them! But the only bread truly blessed is the bread that reminds us of the broken body of our Lord and of His pain.

The sculptures of Michelangelo thrill art lovers all over the world. They are moved by the grace of his "David," but he never signed it. They are awed by the majesty of his "Moses," but he never signed it. They are thunderstruck at the impact of the "Medici Tomb," but he never signed it. The only sculpture he ever signed is the "Pieta"—Mary taking Jesus down from the cross. The only work that bears his name is the one that reflects the crucifixion.

Someone published a book picturing the many shapes of the cross. It has been stylized in a dozen ways. There is a Latin cross, a Greek cross, an Egyptian cross, a Jerusalem cross, a cross of St. Andrew, and an iron cross. Artists and architects have modified its basic form in many ways. I suppose that does no harm, but we must never modify the *meaning* of the cross—Christ died for our sins!

The largest cross in the world is located on Bald Knob mountain in southern Illinois. It towers 111 feet high and can be seen for miles in every direction. But the true cross towers higher. It towers above our vain ambition. It towers above our petty concerns. It towers above all that is fleshly, material, or worldly. It towers above life itself!

A little African boy in Kenya cut his foot badly. Without telling his family, he went at once to the mission hospital. Later, his mother showed up. When asked how she found him, she replied, "I followed the blood."

The nation of Panama was a diplomatic creation of the United States in order to build the Panama Canal. Panama seceded from Columbia without the loss of a single life, except for one man in a laundry killed when a Columbian gunboat lobbed a token shell into the city of Panama! Our spiritual freedom was not so easily won. No accidental death brought it about. It took the deliberate and willing sacrifice of Christ our Lord.

59

When we built Boulder Dam (now Hoover Dam), it was the largest in the world. As is common on such projects, there were the inevitable accidents and some workmen lost their lives. When the dam was complete, they put a plaque into the wall. On it they inscribed the names of the workmen who had died during construction. The plaque begins, "These died that the desert might rejoice and blossom as the rose." So Christ died that the dry and arid souls of men might be refreshed and renewed and turned from total waste to useful service.

A visitor to Russia was walking down the Moscow River at evening. The sun was sinking and its direct rays no longer reached the valley, nor the walls of the Kremlin, nor the palace of the Czars, nor the Soviet flag above it, but shone only on the cross on top of the Church of the Assumption, the old church where the Czars had been crowned. The light lingered last on that cross as if to say that there was something in that cross that would endure when all human institutions had passed away, all Czars had been forgotten, when the last Communist had disappeared and the doctrines of Karl Marx had turned to dust. It suggested to him that the cross would eternally hold meaning and hope for the human race.

When Bomilcar was crucified in the marketplace at Carthage, he shouted curses from his cross and hurled insults at his enemies. When Jesus was crucified on Calvary, He prayed for His enemies: "Father, forgive them, for they know not what they do." Because of His sinless character, Christ's cross has an efficacy that none other possesses. His alone can provide forgiveness of sin.

When the Unknown Soldier was laid to rest in Arlington, he was given the Congressional Medal of Honor and the Croix de Guerre; and to these each of the Allied powers added its highest honor. He was the first non-British citizen to receive the United Kingdom's highest honor. Thus decorated, the body of the Unknown Soldier was laid to rest.

But when the Captain of our salvation was laid to rest, He knew no such pomp and ceremony. The only honor accorded Him by men was Pilate's crude title above the cross: Jesus of Nazareth, King of the Jews. God, however, gave Him a stirring salute, for the earth quaked, darkness shrouded the midday sun; and in His honor, graves were opened and the dead walked. In the face of such honors, the centurion said, "Truly this man was the Son of God." How poor are the honors we come to bestow on Him today. But if we bring with those humble honors lives dedicated to Him, they will be graciously accepted.

When General Douglas MacArthur left the Philippines in the early part of World War II, he made a short speech: "I will return." Later on in the war, he came back to the Philippines in victory. Cameras recorded his wading ashore. He made another speech: "I have returned." The first speech would have been worthless without the second, which gave it force and meaning. So Jesus promised to rise from the dead. How hollow that would sound if He had not come back from the dead. But what a note of victory it now sounds—now that He is risen!

Because he led the army that liberated the Philippines in ✝ World War II, General Douglas MacArthur has been ever since a hero in that country. To this very day, whenever a group of Philippine soldiers answer roll call, after the last name has been called, they always add, "Douglas MacArthur," and someone always answers, "Here!" When we call the roll of the church on earth, Christ is really here. It is not symbolic. It is not a gesture. Because He rose from the dead, He can and does keep His promise, "Lo, I am with you alway." It is not some imposter who answers "Here." He *is* here!

Charles Revlon, president of Revlon Cosmetics, is reported to have said, "I sell hope." Of course, hope can never be bought. It is given away, by Christ, to those who believe!

"It is a poor tale in which humanity slaps at the face of Divinity and gets away with it."

QUOTATIONS

The resurrection of Jesus has given us, as Christians, a new perspective on death. Preaching on the resurrection often comments on that perspective, and may thus find useful some of the following quotations. They reveal much about their authors' views of death, as well as their hope, or hopelessness, for beyond.

Perhaps death is life and life is death,
And victuals and drink an illusion of the senses;
For what is Death but an eternal sleep?
And does not Life consist in sleeping and eating?
                              —Aristophanes

But whether on the scaffold high
    Or in the battle's van,
The fittest place where man can die
    Is where he dies for man!
                              —Michael Joseph Barry

Click, click, click . . . Death is prancing;
Death, at midnight, goes a-dancing,
Tapping on a tomb with talon thin,
Click, click, click, goes the grisly violin.
                              —Henri Cazalis (Jean Lahors)

Things have a terrible permanence
When people die.
                              —Aline (Mrs. Joyce) Kilmer

From wind to wind, earth has one tale to tell;
All other sounds are dulled, and drowned, and lost,
    In this one cry, "Farewell."
                              —Celia Laighton Thaxter

When we have thrown off this old suit,
    So much in need of mending,
To sink among the naked mute,
    Is that, think you, our ending?
                              —George Meredith

But once put out thy light,
Thou cunning'st pattern of excelling nature,
I know not where is that Promethean heat
That can thy light relume.

—Shakespeare

Nothing exists which the British bourgeoisie
Does not understand;
Therefore there is no death
—And, of course, no life.

—Sir Osbert Sitwell

Death is the ugly fact which Nature has to hide, and she hides it
well.

—Alexander Smith

Yes, death is strong, but look you, the strongest,
Stronger is music than death.

—Franz Werfel

Death in itself is nothing; but we fear
To be we know not what, we know not where.

—John Dryden

Afraid? Of whom am I afraid?
Not death; for who is he?
The porter of my father's lodge
As much abasheth me.

—Emily Dickinson

Somewhere I read, in an old book whose name
    Is gone from me, I read that when the days
Of a man are counted, and his business done,
    There comes up the shore at evening, with the tide,
To the place where he sits, a boat—
    And in the boat, from the place where he sits; he sees,
Dim in the dusk, dim and yet so familiar,
    The faces of his friends long dead; and knows
They come for him, brought in upon the tide,
    To take him where men go at set of day.

—Theodore Roosevelt

Neither the sun nor death can be looked at steadily.
                              —Francois, Duc de la Rochefoucauld

As one looks on a face through a window, through life
    I have looked on God.
Because I have loved life, I shall have no sorrow to die.
                              —Amelia Josephine Burr

Death, be not proud, though some have called thee
Mighty and dreadful, for thou art not so:
For those whom thou think'st thou dost overthrow
Die not, poor Death; nor yet canst thou kill me.
                              —John Donne

Why fear death? Death is only a beautiful adventure.
    —(Last words of a passenger to a group of friends as the
        Lusitania was sinking [May 7, 1915] reported by a survivor,
        Rita Jolivet)

Oh, write of me, not "Died in bitter pains,"
But "Emigrated to another star!"
                              —Helen Hunt Jackson

It must be so—Plato, thou reasonest well!
Else whence this pleasing hope, this fond desire,
This longing after immortality?
Or whence this secret dread, and inward horror
Of falling into naught? Why shrinks the soul
Back to herself, and startles at destruction?
'Tis the divinity that stirs within us;
'Tis Heaven itself that points out an hereafter,
And intimates eternity to man.
Eternity! thou pleasing, dreadful thought!
                              —Joseph Addison

EPITAPHS

Lorenzo Savin, 1877, age 74, Eastport, Maine:
Transplanted.

Francis Magranis, 1891, age 85, South Hadley, Massachusetts:
My shoes are made
My work is done;
Yes, dear friends,
I'm going home.
And where I've gone
And how I fare
There's nobody to know
And nobody to care.

Newbury, Massachusetts:
Here lies
In a state of perfect oblivion
John Adams
who died Sept 2 1811
AE 79
Death has decomposed him
And at the great resurrection Christ
will recompose him.

Phineas G. Wright, 1918, age 89, Putnam, Connecticut:
Going, But Know Not Where

East Derry, New Hampshire:
Lizzie James
wife of
Edmund R. Angell
1849-1932
"I don't know how to die."

Jaffrey, New Hampshire:
Sacred to the Memory of Violate
by purchase the slave of Amos Fortune
by marriage his wife, by her
fidelity his companion and solace
She died his Widow Sept. 13, 1802 AEt. 73

Jaffrey, New Hampshire:
    Sacred to the Memory of Amos Fortune
    who was born free in Africa
    a slave in America, he purchased
    liberty, professed Christianity,
    lived reputably, died hopefully
        Nov. 17, 1901 AEt. 91.

Patience Holmes, 1845, age 24, Plymouth, Massachusetts (and
others in New Hampshire and Vermont):
    Shed not for her the bitter tear
    Nor give the heart to vain regret
    'Tis but the casket that lies here
    The gem that filled it sparkles yet.

COMPLETE SERMONS

CROSS WORDS

A minister gave this advice to fellow preachers: "In promulgating your esoteric cogitations, assiduously eschew polysyllabic interjections." That means, "Use small words." We all prefer small words, and I prefer to use them—largely because they are the ones I can understand. But some subjects are so large they demand large words. Such is the case with the cross. Coming here, we must speak of "atonement" and "propitiation," of "reconciliation" and "redemption." The Bible uses such terms. In Romans 5:9-11, we have the word "atonement." John uses a synonym, "propitiation." The idea is the same, balancing the books. Sin created a debt that the cross somehow paid. The cross satisfied the demands of Divine justice.

When the first sin was committed, God slew an animal to make a covering for Adam and Eve. Throughout the Old Testament, lambs were slain on the Day of Atonement. Man is prohibited from eating blood, commanded not to spill blood. Finally, we come to 1 Peter 1:18 and 19 and read of the precious blood of Christ.

How did Christ's death pay the debt? To whom was it paid? Those are questions we cannot understand. It is not necessary to understand it. It is necessary to proclaim it. Christ died in our place. It was vicarious, to use another large word. Christ's suffering was in our stead. No matter how little we can comprehend it, this much is plain. We share the guilt for the death of Christ. We share the good from the death of Christ. We need no other sacrifice. Four times in Hebrews, the writer says Christ died once—"once for all!"

Redemption speaks of freeing the enslaved. That word is not in our text, but the idea is there. We were in bondage to sin. We were like indentured servants who had so indebted themselves to the devil that they must now be his bondservants. We were in bondage to the law. It laid upon us a thousand commandments. A man could never keep all those rules. He might only lean upon a wall and become so unclean he could not go to worship because on the other side of that wall was a dead body. One could never live up to such a law.

Our bondage is illustrated by the forty-seven miners trapped in a gold mine in California. When the rescuers reached them they were dead. In the richest room in the world they suffocated; they were trapped. So sin traps us in the pleasures and riches and cares of this world. A man in New Haven, Connecticut, died recently, in the same room in which he was born. He had never slept in any other room. Think of living all of one's life in a single room! Yet sin so enslaves us, so traps us, that we never see the far spiritual horizons of life. From that bondage Christ sets us free!

Reconciliation. That word looms large in our text. The re-uniting of the separated; man separated from God and, because of that, separated from his fellowman. The cross reunites both. Recently, a door was broken in a Sunday School classroom, split down the middle. Until a new one could be bought, the custodian nailed the broken pieces together again. That is what happened on the cross. Christ literally nailed back together the shattered and broken fragments of our world.

Addison Leitch tells about a trip to Egypt. Along the coast he was shown the spot where a young girl got into trouble in the water. Two young men, missionaries, plunged in to save her. By some strange circumstance, they both drowned, but she was saved. Don't you wonder how she felt? You know how she felt! It happened to you—at Golgotha. Imagine coming to that place years afterward and finding that girl, grown to woman-hood, her life wasted in trifles or in sin. We would ask, "Was her life worth the sacrifice of those others?" And what if we waste our lives—lives bought at so great a sacrifice!

CROSS ROADS

In most every American congregation there is probably someone who has visited Israel and walked the road that Jesus walked to the cross. However, the great majority in any congregation have not done that and will likely never do that. Far more important than walking that road physically, we each need to walk that road spiritually.

"But made himself of no reputation, and took upon him the form of a servant, and was made in the likeness of men: and being found in fashion as a man, he humbled himself, and became obedient unto death, even the death of the cross. Wherefore, God also hath highly exalted him, and given him a name which is above every name: that at the name of Jesus every knee should bow, of things in heaven, and things in earth, and things under the earth."

(Philippians 2:7-10)

Jesus walked the road of humility. For most of us, that is a little-used path. We are too concerned with ego and vanity. Think of what it meant for the Christ who created the world to live upon it and die upon it! Think what it meant for the Christ who created man to die for man. Can we walk that road of humility with him? Each Easter, on Good Friday, the bishop of the Syrian Orthodox Church washes the feet of the choir boys!

Jesus walked the road of obedience. No longer is obedience prized as it once was. There is a new permissiveness in the home. We have discarded the old advice of one who said, "If your child annoys you, soothe him by brushing his hair. If that doesn't work, use the other end of the brush on the other end of the child."

A candidate had gone up into the mountains to garner votes. After talking to a farmer, he turned to the gangling boy who stood nearby. "How about you? Will you vote for me, too?"

"I can't vote."

"Why, you look like you're twenty-one to me."

"I used to be, but I didn't bow my head when Pa asked the blessin', and he set me back two years."

There is a new permissiveness in the home and in the

school. Even in the military, that one institution that seemed to depend upon discipline, there is a new permissiveness. In such an age we may forget that God prizes obedience. He expects to be taken seriously. He intends for us to do His will. "Obedience is better than sacrifice," said God. Jesus walked the road of obedience. "My meat is to do the will of Him that sent me."

Jesus walked the road of sacrifice. We run two extremes when it comes to sacrifice. Some deny themselves for the sake of self-denial. What they sacrifice has no relationship to anything moral or spiritual. That is the worship of will power, not the worship of God. Some run to the other extreme. They say that one ought not deny himself anything that pleases. How hard it is to walk with Jesus the road of meaningful sacrifice.

We have been thinking of roads *to* the cross. They are not dead end streets. There is also a road that leads *from* the cross. We go by the cross on the way to somewhere else. For Jesus, the road from the cross led to His exaltation. So says our text. After the cross came the resurrection. Then when Jesus had appeared to His followers for forty days, He ascended to the right hand of the Father. The road led from the cross to the crown.

That crown He would share with you. Jesus wants you to join Him in His exaltation. To do that you must first join Him on His cross. You do this by turning away from sin. "Our old man is·crucified with Him," says Romans 6:6. When we turn from the old life, we climb upon that cross with Jesus and join Him there.

CROSS PURPOSES

The day was November 9, 1965. It was the night of the great power failure. The lights went out in New York City, Albany, Rochester, Boston, Montreal, Ottawa, and Toronto. Eighty thousand square miles were plunged into darkness, thirty million people affected.

But what is that compared to the darkness that fell in the eighteenth year of Tiberius at Jerusalem, when midnight came at noon. For three hours, an impenetrable darkness shrouded the earth as a carpenter from Nazareth hung on a cross. That darkness was occasioned by no power failure. Quite the contrary. Spiritual power had won the victory over military, political, and religious power put together. Here is the strange truth. In that darkness, the light of God's purpose is most clearly seen. Those purposes are made plain in 1 Peter 1:18-23:

> "Forasmuch as ye know that ye were not redeemed with corruptible things, as silver and gold, from your vain conversation received by tradition from your fathers; but with the precious blood of Christ, as of a lamb without blemish and without spot: who verily was fore-ordained before the foundation of the world, but was manifest in these last times for you, who by him do believe in God, that raised him up from the dead, and gave him glory; that your faith and hope might be in God. Seeing ye have purified your souls in obeying the truth through the Spirit unto unfeigned love of the brethren, see that ye love one another with a pure heart fervently: being born again, not of corruptible seed, but of incorruptible, by the word of God, which liveth and abideth forever."

Here we see that the cross is related to God's eternal purpose. It was planned before the foundation of the world. Revelation 13:8 speaks of the Lamb slain before the foundation of the world. Of course, Christ was not literally slain before the foundation of the world. The meaning must be that God knew about it before creation. How remarkable that He created us at all. Would parents ever become parents if they knew the heartache and the pain it would cause? Perhaps, but no young couple thinks of those things, nor can see that far ahead. God knew, yet He created us.

It means that Christ knew when He came into the world He must die for it. Yet He came. Thus Christ's death is unique. He was immortal. All others who have died sacrificial deaths have been mortal. They would have died eventually anyway. Here one immortal accepts death. His motive was pure mercy. He did not die to gain relief or release, nor for the satisfaction of doing one's duty. It was mercy alone that motivated Him. And He died to procure something for His killers. Many have died for family or country. Christ died for the men who caused His death! "Greater love hath no man than this, that he lay down his life for his friends." Underline the word "man." There is a greater love. Christ died for his enemies.

A Russian novel describes a nobleman driving across the frigid country side, pursued by hungry wolves. One of the horses is left behind, but soon the wolves have devoured him and again are in pursuit. Finally, the servant volunteers to stay behind and to sacrifice himself to give the nobleman time to flee. It was an heroic deed, but the servant offered himself for one whom he regarded as his superior. Here it is the Superior who dies for the inferior.

The cross is related to God's redemptive purpose. It enabled God to save us. Romans 3:25, 26 says that it made it possible for God to be just and the justifier of them that believe. How could a holy God forgive our sin without losing some of His holiness? How could a loving God not offer us forgiveness and yet remain a God of love? Those two dilemmas are solved by the cross.

There is no parallel to it, no illustration of it. It is unique, and nothing like the death of Christ ever happened before or since. The closest we can come is the sacrificial lamb offered in the Old Testament. The Bible uses that comparison, calling Christ the Lamb of God. But even then the differences are greater than the similarities. The lamb stands for innocence and purity, but it is symbolic. The lamb has no moral choice. Jesus did have such a choice, yet He was sinless and pure. The lamb was passive, not willfully going to sacrifice. Christ said, "No man taketh my life from me. I lay it down of myself." There was no personal bond between the lamb and the sinner. Yet Christ was like us, made like unto His brethren.

We are baffled when we see good and evil locked in mortal combat. Christ had a double agony, for He was perfect God and perfect man. As man, He identified with sinners, the victim of Satan. As God, He resisted sin and refused Satan. As man, He felt the divine wrath and displeasure the sinful must always feel in the presence of the holy. As God, He felt the horror the holy must always feel in the presence of sin.

We are in one respect like the British author, DeQuincy. He was a man who turned on to drugs long before the present generation discovered them. He never cleaned the rooms where he lived. When they became uninhabitable, he simply moved on, leaving the mess for someone else to clean up. Because we could do no other, we had to turn over to God the mess that sin had made in our lives. Only He could clean it up.

There are certainly practical purposes to the cross. Everyone reacts to it. Some react with pity, but Christ does not want your pity. "Do not weep for me," He said to the women along the road to Golgotha. Why doesn't He want your pity? Because it reverses the whole plan. God pities man, not the reverse; the cross was His destiny. "For this purpose came I into the world." It was "for the joy set before Him" that He endured the cross. Pity suggests weakness, but here is strength. Most of all, pity can get in the way of the larger emotions Christ wants you to feel—worship, adoration, commitment.

To the Greeks the cross was foolishness, to the Jews a stumbling block. What is it to you? It should be a convincing demonstration of love. "Herein is love," wrote John, "Not that we loved God, but that He loved us and sent His son to be the propitiation for our sins." Paul agrees saying, "God commendeth his love toward us, in that, while we were yet sinners, Christ died for us."

Here is a strong affirmation that the purposes of God cannot be thwarted. Certainly the cross was a wicked scheme conceived in evil hearts; but God foresaw their plans. And in making them, they played into the very hand of God. They tried to silence Him with a cross, but that cross became the sounding board to send the gospel around the world.

Here is a powerful example of patience, of suffering, of obedience. So Peter sees it in 1 Peter 2:21-24. Two Moravian missionaries once entered a leper colony with the gospel, knowing that if they went in, they could never come out again.

What inspires such dedication? Two others, in the West Indies, found no way to reach the slaves on a large plantation; so they sold themselves into slavery that they might preach to them. What inspires such sacrifice? It is Christ upon His cross.

The cross has an appealing invitation. Never is there a revival without a sermon on the cross. Never is there an evangelistic sermon that does not somewhere touch upon the cross. Turn through the hymnal. The most appealing songs are songs of the cross. The cross will bring out the best in us—or the worst in us. The cross brought out the best in John. Who would have thought that shy, quiet John should be the only one of the twelve with enough courage to stand by the cross. The cross brought out the best in Mary, and the other women, in the centurion, in Nicodemus. The cross brought out the worst in Pilate, Herod, Judas, the soldiers. Why do you suppose they mocked Him and spat upon Him?

The cross is the great divider. It sorts people out. It sifts them. Look at those two thieves on Calvary. They looked just alike to everyone. No one thought there was any difference in them. But the cross separated them and showed us a tremendous difference. So the cross sifts us, sorts us out—brings out our best or our worst. That outstretched arm would touch your life today.

> "Let me no more my comfort draw
>   From my frail hold on thee.
> In this alone rejoice with awe;
>   Thy mighty grasp of me."

THE VIEW AT CALVARY

I wonder how those who stood at Calvary and watched Jesus die felt about what they saw. Today we can sing so casually, "I will cherish the old rugged cross," or, "Beneath the cross of Jesus, I fain would take my stand." Without blinking an eye, we can sing, "Jesus, keep me near the cross. . . . Bring its scenes before me." Could those who gathered around Calvary have sung, "Bring its scenes before me"? I suspect that as they saw what happened at that place of horror, they might have said, "Take these scenes from me. I never want to think of them again." Luke's gospel tells us:

> And all the people that came together to that sight, beholding the things which were done, smote their breasts, and returned. And all his acquaintance, and the women that followed him from Galilee, stood afar off, beholding these things. (Luke 23:48, 49)

Yes, I am sure it was a day that they wanted to forget. But they didn't forget. They began to meet together and remember His death every first day of the week. The apostle Paul would even say, "For I determined not to know anything among you, save Jesus Christ, and him crucified" (1 Corinthians 2:2). As the facts began to come together for them, they began to think of Calvary as often as they could.

We, too, must make a pilgrimage to Calvary. If we are going to see what they saw, then we are going to have to look, even though the scenes are not pleasant. We must look upon the view at Calvary. Only there can we grasp certain essential truths. Only there can the most important facts of history be presented to us in a dramatic and unforgettable way.

At Calvary, we see Christ's righteousness despised! It was despised by the Jews and their leaders. They had been waiting for the Holy One of God; but when they beheld His holiness, they despised it. How sad that many Jews were unable to accept the very one they had been waiting and praying for.

Christ's righteousness was despised by the Romans. They were not involved in the religious debate over Jesus; yet they found cause to mock Him. Was there something in Jesus' attitude that the callous Romans could not understand? These

Romans admired power; and perhaps they could not appreciate this one who stood as a sheep stands dumb before the shearers.

Christ's righteousness was even despised by one of His own disciples. Judas, who was at one time a trusted confidant, saw Christ as one to be bartered. How ironic that the one most worthy of our highest praise was subjected to our lowest humiliation.

When Mahatma Ghandi, the great advocate of the non-violent protest, was gunned down by an assassin, someone said, "Now we know how dangerous it is to be good." We see that point even clearer in Christ. The only place this world has for people like Jesus is on crosses.

We also see Christ's righteousness displayed. Here in the most trying time of His life we see His holiness shine through. Moments of trial tend to accent the best and worst in a person. In Christ, we see His goodness so clearly that we stand in awe. There is only goodness in Him.

His righteousness was displayed in His attitude toward His enemies. Would anyone have blamed Jesus for some few sarcastic words to those who conspired to put Him to death? Yet, Jesus showed only compassion for His enemies and asked the Father for their forgiveness. Earlier in His ministry, Jesus had talked about loving our enemies. We might have thought that His words were an unattainable ideal if He hadn't shown us how to love our enemies.

His righteousness was displayed in His attitude toward His friends. When we are in a time of great need, we hope our friends will support us. At Calvary, we do not see Jesus' friends supporting Him—we see Jesus supporting His friends.

Christ's righteousness was displayed in His attitude toward suffering. Jesus accepts suffering. He realizes that no one can escape it. Jesus did not come to the cross cheerfully. If He had, we would have wondered about His sanity. No one enjoys suffering, not even the Lord. He did, however, accept suffering. He faced it in a way that inspires us all.

Christ's righteousness was displayed in His attitude toward death. Jesus wanted to avoid Calvary, but it wasn't because He was afraid to die. He might have been reluctant to face the pain of death. He might have wanted to live longer. He wasn't afraid to die. Listen to His final words: "Father, into thy hands I commend my spirit." What a beautiful way to look at death. When we die, we are placing ourselves in the hands of the Father.

We can look at Calvary and see the actions of Christ. Surely, we are led to say, "Thou art the Christ, the son of the living God."

We aren't the only ones to be affected by the scenes of Calvary. We have seen Christ's righteousness despised and Christ's righteousness displayed. Now, let us see Christ's righteousness declared.

Christ's righteousness was declared by Pilate. He said, "I find no fault in Him." Though he did not, as far as we know, believe in Jesus, Pilate knew a good person when he saw one. Though he did not have the courage to set Christ free, he could not bear to judge this Holy One.

Christ's righteousness was declared by the centurion. He said, "Truly this man was the Son of God." Admittedly, his faith was partial and incomplete; but he was strongly touched by the man on the cross.

Nature even declared Christ's righteousness. When Jesus died, all of God's fury was set loose upon Calvary. There was darkness and an earthquake. It was as if God's anger could be held back no more. The temple veil came apart. Surely a nagging thought crept into many minds: "What have we done?"

God didn't finish there. Three days later came the ultimate declaration of Christ's righteousness. The Father raised Him from the dead. This, the most dramatic and startling event in history, was done so that God could say once again, "This is my beloved Son." Only after the resurrection did the meaning of the cross become clear. This Jesus and His execution might have faded from memory without the resurrection. After He had risen, they could look back at the cross and comprehend it.

So, the disciples took this message with them. They declared to the world what they had seen. Down through the centuries the message of Jesus, who conquered sin and death, has been passed on.

So it comes to all—a compulsion to go to Calvary. People long to go to Jerusalem and see the place where Jesus died. It is, indeed, a moving experience. But it is far more important to come spiritually to Calvary. After our spiritual pilgrimage to Calvary, we will leave changed. At Calvary, our eyes grow moist and our throat becomes choked with emotion. Maybe then we can understand the spirit of that great hymn that says:

> When I survey the wondrous cross,
> On which the Prince of glory died,
> My richest gain I count but loss,
> And pour contempt on all my pride.
>
> Were the whole realm of nature mine,
> That were a present far too small;
> Love so amazing, so divine,
> Demands my soul, my life, my all.

THE INDISPENSABLE ACT OF GOD

Situated on the narrow isthmus between the Ionian and Aegean seas, the city of Corinth, and hence the church that was established there, occupied a strategic position in the Roman world. Paul's first letter to this divided, disturbed congregation occupies an equally strategic position in the New Testament library. The apostle opened that letter with a discussion of the gospel, moved to instructions for Christian living, and finally to the ordinances that fortify our faith and the works that demonstrate it. In Chapter 15, he undergirded all that goes before, showing that the resurrection is the key to Christian living, the keynote of the Christian gospel, and the keystone of Christian faith. This chapter, then, is the climax of the letter.

When we examine 1 Corinthians 15, we can readily see why it has come to be regarded as a masterpiece of sacred literature. It declares that the resurrection of Jesus from the dead is the paramount, the climactic, the indispensable act of God.

From Paul's viewpoint, the gospel was more than a picture to be admired. It was a tool to be used. The gospel was that by which men are saved and wherein they stand.

To the zoologist, one thing that distinguishes man from the rest of the animal kingdom is his ability to stand erect. To Paul, the man of God is distinguished from the man of the world by his ability to stand against the devil's wiles.

He said just that in the letter to the Ephesians, describing the Christian soldier, who stands his ground against seemingly hopeless odds. Such a description is reminiscent of the handful of brave Greeks who stood at Thermopylae and held that pass against a horde of invading Persians. Their heroism made possible "the glory that was Greece." It reminds us of Concord Bridge, where "once the embattled farmers stood and fired the shot heard round the world."

Ours is a similar situation. Satan has set out to invade the domain of God. He storms the citadels of our hearts and day after day lays seige to our souls. We must stand firm. To do so, we must have something on which to stand. Paul says we can plant our feet firmly on the solid rock of the empty tomb. The resurrection is God's assurance that the battle must eventually be His—and ours! Victory is certain. God turned the tide at the empty tomb! It is only a matter of time until that victory is secured. In that interim, we must hold the fort, guard the pass, stand our ground.

It is not enough to stand against something. We must also stand for something. Wise is the old adage, "He who does not stand for something is apt to fall for anything." Our militant posture must be more than defensive. One thinks at once of Martin Luther, pleading for freedom of conscience, "Here I stand. I cannot do otherwise. God help me." That unswerving stand altered forever the course of human history. J.R. Lowell wrote of it:

What! Shall one monk scarce known beyond
    his cell
Front Rome's far-reaching bolts and
    scorn her frown?
Brave Luther answered *yes;* that
    thunder's swell
Rocked Europe, and discharmed the
    triple crown.

We, too, must have principles we will not compromise at any cost. We must have values we will never surrender. Someone has remarked that in our day no one seems wholly and irrevocably committed to anything. Such commitment seems unreasonable, fanatic, foolish. The theme song of the church is no longer, "Stand up, stand up for Jesus, ye soldiers of the cross." Now it seems to be, "For he's a jolly good fellow," or "Hail, hail, the gang's all here." Let us sing again, "The fight is on," and mean it!

To remember the resurrection is to be reminded of the faithfulness of God. What a contrast it is to man's faithlessness, and how it inspires him to greater loyalty! To remember the resurrection is to be reminded of God's power. How weak is man without Him; how strong if He is near!

To remember His resurrection is to recall our own, when in baptism we were buried with Him. We participated in the likeness of His resurrection that we might walk in newness of life. Is our life really new? Are the old sins still there? Do we still walk in the old ways? Are we like the alien who has come to live in a new land, but will not learn its language nor live by its customs?

Our commemoration of the resurrection reminds us that

the old man is crucified and buried, and that he must not be disinterred. It re-emphasizes that from that grave God raised up a new man, who is truly after His own image.

More than this, the resurrection is the key to Christian living because it assures us that we serve a living Lord. He is by our side. He sees us falter. He hears our uncomely speech. He knows our un-Christian thoughts. Surely the good news that Christ lives will motivate us to higher and holier lives. Surely the mighty act of God in raising up Jesus will also lift us up and let us stand "by faith on Heaven's tableland." It is a living Christ who plants our feet on higher ground.

In a symphony, every note on the keyboard may at times be used; but the harmony will be determined by a single combination that sets the tone and determines the harmonic arrangment of the whole. In the chapter before us, Paul declares that three facts constitute the dominant chord of the gospel; and by devoting fifty-four of the chapter's fifty-eight verses to the third fact, he leaves no doubt that it is the keynote.

These essential facts are that Christ died, that He was buried, and that He rose again. It is not correct to say that they are the gospel, for they alone do not exhaust the gospel. Paul only contends that they are indispensable to the gospel; that without them there can be no gospel.

There is a note of sacrifice. Christ died. What could possibly be good about news like that? What sort of man could sing joyfully of the death of another, could say, "In the cross of Christ I *glory?*"

What is so glorious about death? Christ's death finds its glory in the fact that He died "for our sins." His death, then, was something more than heroic, something more than innocent and undeserved, something more even than vicarious.

Only Christ could have gone to the cross with the innocence of a child and with the self-determination of a man. Only He stood in full command of His powers, yet innocent of any sin. There had been before, and have been since, innocent deaths and willing deaths. But never before such a combination of the two!

His death for our sins was "according to the Scriptures." The shadow of the cross hangs unmistakably over the Old Testament. While only glimpsed in Genesis, its outline is clearly visible in the psalms of David and in the prophecies of Zechariah, Isaiah, and Daniel. Every minute detail of these predictions was fulfilled, from the manner of death to the place of burial. Thus seen, the crucifixion becomes more than the mad scheme of heartless men. It becomes the pre-meditated plan of a loving God, and the determined purpose of a compassionate Christ.

There is a note of satisfaction. As has already been inti-mated, the dominant one of these three notes is the final one, the resurrection. But that event rests squarely upon the other two. Pointing to an empty tomb means nothing, unless you can establish that a man, once dead, was buried there.

Paul does not bother to prove that "Christ was buried." He assumes that the assertion will go undisputed, as it did until recent times. After all, what else could you do with a body in the hot climate of Palestine? Without the embalming skill of Egypt, or the refrigeration of modern times, what alternatives existed? Why, then, does Paul even mention it, let alone place it between the cardinal events of death and resurrection? He does so to satisfy our minds regarding Christ's death.

Suppose that He did not really die. Suppose that He expe-rienced a coma on the cross. While this theory is hardly a credit to the discernment of His executioners, it recurs from time to time. Let us suppose it to be correct. Would then the embalmers not have discovered it? Would not the tomb have stifled Him? Would not the soldiers on guard have prevented His escape? The fact that he was buried is important because it reaches in two directions to validate both His death and His resurrection.

The empty tomb, then, has become the world's most elo-quent witness to the resurrection. Its mute testimony remains to this day unanswered and unanswerable. "He is not here." Try every possible explanation. Only one is reasonable. His friends would not have stolen the body, for they did not expect a resurrection. His enemies would not have taken it, for they placed a guard to keep it. He could not have merely swooned at Golgotha; for then the soldiers would have fin-ished on Sunday morning the work they did not complete on Friday.

How significant is that seal the Romans placed upon the tomb! While it did not keep the door shut, the fact that it was placed there seals forever, with even higher authority, the doorway of doubt and makes the resurrection the only possible explanation for His reappearance.

There is a note of certainty. Paul takes great pains to prove the resurrection. To him, the justification of the saint, the judgment of the sinner, and the hope of immortality all rest upon it. Said he, "If thou shalt confess with thy mouth the Lord Jesus, and shalt believe in thine heart *that God hath raised Him from the dead,* thou shalt be saved." At Athens, he said that God "hath appointed a day, in which he will judge the world in righteousness by that man whom he hath ordained; whereof *he hath given assurance unto all men, in that he hath raised him from the dead."*

From the sepulchral bench in Joseph's tomb, Jesus goes to the judicial bench in eternity's courtroom. Only those who have confessed Him here will He confess there.

How important become those words, "I believe that Jesus is the Christ, the Son of the living God." While that confession is brief and general, the faith that lies behind it must be detailed and specific. Paul could not have accepted the contention that to acknowledge Jesus as Lord was all that mattered. To him, belief in the resurrection, a specific event, was vital, central, irreplaceable—so much so that it gave assurance of both salvation and judgment!

To give certainty to the claim, Paul calls forth his witnesses. The number of them is "above five hundred." For him and for us, there need be no note of uncertainty in the playing of this symphony. We need not soft-pedal its claims, lest they be found false. We can mark it fortissimo and sound the diapason of deliverance with complete assurance. "Christ the Lord is risen today, Alleluia!"

A stone arch is a wonder to behold. What holds the stones in place, with nothing but the thin air beneath? The answer is the keystone. Of a different size and shape, and placed in its strategic position at the top of the arch, it holds all of the other stones together.

If we think of Christianity as the Arch of Triumph through which the conquering Christ triumphantly marches, then the resurrection of Christ is the keystone in that arch. Without it, all the assembled facts and hopes of our religion crumble and lie shattered at our feet.

To make certain that this stone will remain in place and do well its work, Paul held it up to three tests. He made a prophetic test, an empirical test, and a philosophical test. In 1 Corinthians 15, he declares that the resurrection is made valid by Scripture, by the five senses, and by common sense.

He makes use of the prophetic test by repeating again and again the same refrain, "according to the Scriptures." Old Testament references to the resurrection are few, but they are powerful. Jesus' predictions of His resurrection are even stronger and more specific.

Paul next applies the empirical test: "He was seen." Here is an appeal to the highest order of evidence known to man. All American jurisprudence rests upon it. It is the testimony of witnesses.

Were they competent witnesses, these people to whom Paul referred? They had been with Jesus night and day throughout His ministry. For more than three years, ever since His baptism by John in Jordan, they had walked with Him, talked with Him, eaten with Him, lived with Him. They would have recognized an imposter at once. Their competence is amply demonstrated in the growth of the Christian religion and in the books that they composed.

But competency is not the only test of a witness. Were they honest? Had they anything to gain by making the claims they did? No. They had everything to lose! As one of them put it, "We have forsaken all." These men staked their lives upon this gospel and died for their faith in this Christ.

Were they themselves deceived? Was their conviction of Jesus' having risen perhaps some hallucination, some trick of the mind, triggered by wishful thinking, something conjured up by an overworked imagination?

Hardly. Even a brief consideration of the array of witnesses summoned in this chapter quickly evaporates such an objection. The risen Lord appeard to believers and unbelievers, to individuals and to groups large and small, by night and by day, indoors and out of doors, in the city and in the country, in Judea and Galilee.

His visitation extended over a period of forty days. During this time He walked, talked, and ate in their presence. Of the five senses, at least three tested the contention that He was alive. They saw Him, they heard Him, they touched Him. In every way, He conducted himself no differently from the way He had before. The empirical test says with certainty, "He lives!"

Perhaps the most dramatic part of 1 Corinthians 15 is that in which Paul applies the philosophical test. "If Christ be not raised . . ." he begins. With that conjecture as a launching pad, he transports us into a bleak and forbidding universe where there is no help and no hope for mankind. Appealing to common sense, he shows the strategic and indispensable position the resurrection plays in the Christian system. He is saying, in effect, that if the finest flower of the human race withered and died never to bloom again, what possible hope can there be for the rest of mankind? All our hope, says he, is hinged upon those few dramatic hours between the Sabbath's sunset and sunrise on the first day of the week.

Paul adds that on this dread condition, "your faith is vain." All that man has ever held dear, all that he has cherished about God and self, all his faith, was nothing more than idle speculation. There is no God of omnipotent power, no Christ of unmatched love, no eternity of unending bliss! Faith? It is merely a word to conjure with, a crutch for the weak, a talisman for the foolish. All our goals and ideals are gone. The cupboard of our souls is bare. We must turn for solace, strength, and happiness to the meager reserves of a material world that measures the worth of all things by the yardstick of dollars and cents. Greed must now be our god and materialism our master, and life be forever bound up in the transient pleasures and tinseled possessions of this present world. "If in this life only we have hope. . . ." Who can bear to finish the sentence?

Paul adds to this a still more powerful argument. "If Christ be not raised . . . ye are yet in your sins!"

What man is so insensible that he cannot feel the burden of his sins, so ignorant he cannot read the tally of his own soul's exhausted inventory? The stains of sin are deep, and the awful weight of a single life's wrongdoing is more than man can bear.

Are we now to believe that these stains can never be erased, this burden never lifted, the books of the soul never balanced? Consider what life would be like to live with our guilt day after day, and then to die with its load still lying heavily on our hearts! Under such conditions, who would really want to live forever, here or anywhere?

But if we deny the resurrection, this is the situation we must face and accept—a situation made more poignant when Paul points out that "they also which are fallen asleep in Christ are perished." Never again shall we see the smiling face, hear the familiar voice, be reunited with those we "have loved long since and lost a while."

If the resurrection is not fact—if it is only fancy, fable, or parable—then the road to the grave is a one-way street, and life is a hopeless riddle. With nothing to believe in, nothing to hope for, and nothing to live for, we would be indeed "of all men most miserable." Thank God, it is not in this life only that we have hope in Christ. Thank God this life is, in the words of Paul Scherer "open at both ends, and the winds of eternity blow through it."

Having painted this dark and somber picture of a Christless, lifeless, loveless world, Paul races to assure us that this is not the way things really are at all. In verse 20, he presents an emphatic affirmation that Christ is indeed risen and alive forevermore. Like the sun in our solar system, He has come to take His rightful place as the Son in the spiritual "soular" system of the heart. "But now is Christ risen!" This is no question. It is a positive declaration that removes all the question marks of life and replaces them with exclamation points. "Thanks be to God, which giveth us the victory!"

That victory must find its expression not only in the hereafter, but in the here and now. Paul's conclusion is dramatic and pointed, "Therefore, my beloved brethren, be ye stedfast, unmoveable, always abounding in the work of the Lord, forasmuch as ye know that your labor is not in vain in the Lord."

CHILDREN'S SERMONS

Whether the children's sermon is done in the midst of a regular worship service or separately in a Children's Worship Service, Resurrection Sunday presents a special challenge to preaching to children. Here are some ideas.

The Lily

(Have ready to show the children a lily in full bloom and a dry bulb from which the lily grows.)

Isn't the lily beautiful? But if you could have seen this lily a few months ago you would not have thought it was beautiful at all. It would have looked just like this. *(Hold up bulb.)* It would have looked like this if you could have seen it. But it would have been buried. This ugly, dry bulb, buried in the earth, can produce a lovely lily.

We can think of Jesus as like this lily. His body was dead and lifeless. It was buried, just as a bulb is buried. But on Resurrection morning, He came forth in all His life and beauty.

Because of His resurrection, we know that all Christians who have died will be resurrected, too. Have you ever been to a funeral? A dead body is like this bulb. It is buried in the earth, just as the bulb is planted in the earth. But one day God will raise up from the grave everyone who loves and follows Jesus. We are always sad when people we love die; but we know that we will see them again some day. That is why Resurrection Sunday is such a happy time for all Christians.

"Wings from Worms"

(Secure a mounted butterfly, an imitation butterfly, or a large picture of a butterfly.)

What is more beautiful than a butterfly? Do you know how a butterfly starts his life? He starts as a worm—a wooly, wiggly worm. If you didn't know that it happened, it would be difficult to believe that a worm could turn into a butterfly. But it really does happen.

Death is not a pretty thing. The death of Jesus was the

ugliest death of all. But God made something beautiful out of it. In the resurrection of Jesus, God was doing the same kind of thing He does when He makes butterflies out of worms. We are always sad when people we love die; but we know that God can make something good out of it. Because of Jesus' resurrection, we know it is possible for them to live again, too.

There is something else that is very ugly. It is sin. Sin is the ugliest thing in the world. It is even uglier than death. In fact, sin is so ugly the Bible says it is like death. But the Bible also says that being forgiven for sin is like coming back from the dead, like being resurrected.

When God forgives us for our sins, He makes us into a new creature, just as He makes the new creature of the butterfly out of the old creature of the worm. God does this because He loves us. God does this when we love Him.

"Seedtime and Harvest"

The apostle Paul was writing to some very well educated city folks; and he talked to them about some of the simplest things. He talked to them about seeds. *(Hold up a card with various seeds glued to it.)* He talked to them about seeds because He wanted them to believe in the resurrection of Jesus. Paul knew that you have to use things people know about to explain things they don't know about.

If you didn't know about seeds, you would wonder what a farmer or a gardener was doing burying his seeds in the ground. You would think that that was the end of the seed. But it isn't. After a while, the seed sprouts. A lovely, green plant comes up. It is much larger and much more beautiful than the little seed from which it came.

When people die and are buried, some say that is the end of them. We know better. If those people who died are believers in Jesus Christ, it is not the end. Just like the seed, someday God is going to raise them from the dead. He is going to raise them as certainly as He raised Jesus from the dead.

When he raises them from the dead and they go to Heaven, they will have lovely new bodies. They will be much better than their old bodies, as the plant is more beautiful than the seed. And this resurrection is just as sure to happen as a seed is sure to sprout and grow in your garden. God planned it that way. It is a way He shows how much He loves us.

"When the Seal Was Broken"

(Partially melt parrafin or sealing wax and mold into two irregular lumps. Attach one lump of wax to each end of a cord or string.)

Today, when we think of sealing something, we think of making it air-tight so that it will keep. The seal had a completely different meaning in Jesus' day. When Jesus was buried, His enemies were afraid that His disciples would steal His body and say that Jesus had come back from the dead. So they asked the government to seal the tomb.

That did not mean that they made it air-tight. It simply meant that they should mark it in such a way that it would be known if anyone disturbed it; and it would be a crime if anyone disturbed it. So they took two pieces of wax, like these. They stretched the string across the edge where the stone met the doorway of the tomb. Then they pressed into the wax on either end of the string an impression. The impression was made in the wax which showed the symbols of the Roman government. Then if anybody tampered with it, they were guilty of breaking the law.

The seal didn't make it impossible to move the stone, but it made it a crime to move the stone. Then they put guards to watch the tomb. That way, if anyone did break the seal, they would know at once who it was.

Of course, nothing could keep Jesus in the tomb. He arose. Then angels came and rolled away the stone. They couldn't arrest them! When they rolled the stone away they sat on it! Isn't that a nice touch? They sat on the stone! The stone wasn't rolled away to let Jesus out. It was rolled away to let the disciples in!

'Neath the Old Olive Trees

(Hold up an olive.) This olive came from a tree. There are thousands of olive trees in the land of the Bible. The night before Jesus was crucified, He was very sad. He didn't want to leave His disciples; but He knew He had to go to the cross. He decided to pray. He went with his disciples to a place where there were lots of olive trees. We call it the Garden of Gethsemane. Gethsemane means "oil press." It was the place where the olives were pressed between stones to make olive oil.

When people today go to visit the land of the Bible, they always go to Gethsemane. They usually sing a song like "In the Garden" or " 'Neath the Old Olive Trees." Did you know that there are still olive trees there? They are very old. They have grown up from the roots of the very trees that were there when Jesus was there.

Jesus asked the disciples to wait while he prayed. Some of them fell asleep. Jesus understood, for they were very tired. But the disciples were very ashamed that they had not stayed awake while Jesus prayed.

If we try hard, we can almost see Jesus kneeling on the ground under those olive trees. We can see it in our imagination. One of the things He said there was, "Not my will, but thine be done." We all need to be like Jesus. We need to pray when we are sad or when we have difficult things to do. We need to pray, "Not my will, but Thine be done."

When we pray, God will give us strength. He will help us to do what we have to do, just as He helped Jesus. If someone needs our prayers, we must pray for them.

122
144

PROGRAM
reSOURCES

ATTENDANCE PROMOTIONS

From Galilee to Golgotha

It is approximately seventy-five miles, as the crow flies, from Galilee to Golgotha. Attendance for the six to eight weeks preceding Resurrection Day can be promoted by figuring what you want to average for each Sunday, multiplying it by the number of Sundays, and then dividing that by seventy-five. (Or you could adjust the mileage to seventy or eighty to make it come out evenly.) The resulting figure is the number of people you need to travel one mile. Divide your weekly attendance by that figure to find out how many miles you have gone, traveling with Jesus from Galilee to Golgotha.

For example, let's say you want to average 150 for eight weeks. First, multiply 150 by 8, and you get 1200. Divide this by 75, and you get 16. You need sixteen people in attendance to travel one mile. If you have exactly 150 every week, you will travel 9 3/8 miles each week (150÷16), and in eight weeks you will cover the seventy-five miles.

Again, suppose you want to average 350 for six weeks. Multiply 350 by 6, and you get 2100. Adjust the mileage to seventy for convenience, and divide 2100 by 70. Your answer is 30, which is the number it takes to travel one mile. If you average 350 during the six weeks, you will travel an average of 11 2/3 miles each week (350÷30), or 70 miles during the campaign.

A map of Israel in Bible times or a map of modern Israel could be enlarged to mark and display your progress. Or a large chart could be made showing a road twisting from Galilee to Golgotha. You might want to show some points along the way, like Nazareth and Nain, Shechem, and Bethel. A colorful cut-out of a church can be moved along the path to show progress, or a small head of Christ, or simply a large, round, colorful circle. Another way to show progress would be to leave the path white and color it in as progress is made.

The good thing about such a campaign is that one low Sunday does not destroy the possibility of reaching the goal and can be overcome on a succeeding Sunday. You need a minimum of six weeks to take advantage of the build-up of momentum and for word of the effort to get around. Probably eight weeks is the maximum period in which interest can be sustained.

Golgotha to Galilee

Of course, if you want the attendance campaign to follow Resurrection Day, it is a simple matter to reverse the above procedure since the risen Christ promised to meet His disciples in Galilee. It would not be effective to do both campaigns back to back! Choose whatever period seems best for attendance promotion.

As Far As Bethany

Luke 24:50 says, "He led them out as far as Bethany." This suggests another possibility for a post-Resurrection campaign. Bethany is fifteen furlongs from Jerusalem. The landmarks along the way are the Garden of Gethsemane, the Mount of Olives, Bethpage, the home of Lazarus, and Bethany itself.

Lilies for Our Lord

Another way to promote attendance in observance of the resurrection is to have a large poster or signboard painted with a huge lily minus the blooms. Each Sunday the goal is reached a bloom is painted on, or attached to, the lily.

Rolling Away the Stone

A large poster showing the tomb with the stone in front of the door can be marked in such a way that each Sunday the goal is reached the stone is rolled a little farther back. By Resurrection Sunday, the stone is rolled away completely.

Cross Words

Create a large crossword puzzle with either six or eight words to be inserted, words that have to do with the cross, such as atonement, redemption, reconciliation, new life, grace, lamb, and others. There is a number for each word corresponding to the Sundays of the campaign. The first week, you might fill in number one across if the goal is reached; the next, number two down, and so on. It would be possible to tie this to a series of sermons on each of these important Cross Words.

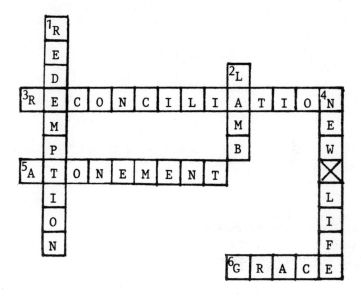

Resurrection to Pentecost

There are eight Sundays from Resurrection to Pentecost; and that is a natural period for an attendance campaign. Perhaps it could be coupled with sermons on the appearances of the risen Lord or other events that lay between these two great events in Christian history.

The Easter Fire

Note the Greek custom of blacking out the church at midnight on Resurrection Saturday and then lighting candles from a single flame lit in the chancel of the church. They call it the "Easter fire." That should be the springboard for a fine post-Resurrection promotion! How long will the "Easter fire" last for us? When will it burn out? You probably should not attempt a real flame for obvious safety reasons, but a simulated flame would do nicely.

BEHIND THE PUBLICITY

Charts and posters help advertise a program and dramatize progress; but there must be more than that for an attendance promotion to work. You will need a structure behind the "window dressing." Some possibilities are:

A telethon to every member

Concerted absentee contact in Sunday School

People sign a commitment card to attend all six Sundays

Guest Day or Each-One-Bring-One or Come Double or Twin Day

Promoters to sign up ten each for one Sunday

Dads and daughters day (with gifts to the look-alikes)

Mother and sons day (again honoring the look-alikes)

Family day (try to have the whole family and recognize the largest)

Cards mailed weekly to all possible attenders

Enrollment drive to reach new people

ONE DAY PROMOTIONS

For Resurrection Day

Nothing works better than promoters who will each sign up ten people to attend. Why not get each promoter one Easter card from the greeting card store and have them sign up attenders on that? If you want to break a record, paint the number on an old record disk and break it publicly. If you have done that, have a huge disk sawed out of plywood and paint the number on it. Then announce you are going to break the biggest record you ever attempted to break!

For after Resurrection Day

Many congregations have done well promoting the Sunday following Easter. It can be called "Easter Plus One." You try to have one more than the Easter total on the Sunday following. This calls for lots of work behind the scenes to line people up to attend. It could be called "Easter Afterglow." Study the customs of the Greek Easter, which is often later than our Easter. You might be able to design a program promoting attendance on "The Second Easter."

STEWARDSHIP PROMOTIONS

Thirty Pieces of Silver

This is an old idea that has been widely used with success. It requires lots of pulpit announcements, posters, a letter to the whole membership, and constant emphasis. Also, it is necessary to provide a bag or other receptacle in which each individual can place his thirty pieces.

Rolling Away the Stone

Look at the attendance campaign with the same name, which is described in this book. A debt elimination campaign could be adapted from that quite easily. While the tie-in to debt is more obvious, any other kind of financial need could be met with a "roll the stone away" campaign. After all, it was rolling away the stone that allowed the disciples to go into the tomb and be convinced of the resurrection.

Forty Days of Faith

Since Jesus appeared to His disciples for a period of forty days after the resurrection, you could construct a campaign to raise any amount of money by dividing it by forty. It could be one dollar for each of the forty days, or five, or ten, or twenty.

SPECIAL COMMUNION SERVICES

As a special observance, try a Passover Seder, with the Lord's Supper as the closing. If that is too ambitious, then have the elements of the Passover feast on a table. Explain the symbolism of the elements and relate it to the Lord's Supper. Then share Communion.

You could re-enact the Last Supper with costumes and scenery, with the congregation participating at the close. If you do not have enough personnel, then try a first-person account in costume as the devotional prior to Communion.

Using slides can enhance Thursday Communion services or Good Friday services. You can use slides from the life of Christ that come from various movie or TV productions. You can use slides that show the same events from great works of art. Holy Land slides could also be used effectively.

A simple but effective Communion service can make use of a cassette program. Pre-record a Communion meditation and devotional music. The entire audience then can commune with the minister and instrumentalists all sharing together. Prior to the opening of the service, the congregation should be instructed to come forward and serve themselves in silence during the musical part of the tape. They should then remain silent as they go to their cars.

Sometimes a special Communion service can be enhanced by the way we use hymns.

"Here Oh My Lord, I See Thee Face to Face" is often used for Communion. Try the first two stanzas before Communion. They focus on Jesus and the meaning of the emblems. Then, after the service, sing the last two stanzas. They speak of the "symbols" disappearing and the feast being over, while the final stanza speaks of the Lord's Supper as a foretaste of the great bridal feast to come.

Another creative way to use a hymn is to sing it a cappella as the emblems are served. This is done effectively as the song leader begins the song after the first couple of rows are served. As each person finishes, he joins the song. There is a gradual crescendo until the entire congregation is singing together.

SPECIAL PROGRAMS

Do you live in a community that has a lake or a beach area? If you do, why not sponsor a Galilean service? Have singers in a boat with a lighted cross. Let the message be delivered from the boat or the shore. This service is common in church camps, but many in your area have never seen it. It can be an inspiring evening to share with your neighbors.

Why not hold a special "Inquirers Class" leading up to a "decision day" in conjunction with the special observance of Christ's resurrection. The class will provide the teaching the prospects need; and the sermon will provide the inspiration to motivate people to make a solid decision.

A special emphasis on the resurrection for young people could include a Homeland-Holyland Tour. Perhaps there are areas in your town that could serve as an acceptable substitute for some sight in the Holy Land. For instance, a lakeside or beach area could suggest the Sea of Galilee. The tallest place in town could suggest the Mount of Olives. A courtroom could serve as Pilate's judgment hall. Your final stop would be a grave yard, an excellent place for a devotional, lesson, or sermon on the resurrection. You will have to be creative and use your imagination. See whether there might not be some "holy sites" in your home town.

Tableaus are often used to observe Christ's birth. Why not have one to observe His resurrection as well? The scenes that could be used include the Last Supper, the prayer in the garden, Judas' betrayal, the judgment hall, Calvary, and the tomb. This would need to be adapted, depending on such things as your church's facilities, membership, and talent. They could be done "live" with church people posing in an appropriate scenery. Or the whole thing could be done months in advance and photographed for a slide presentation at the appropriate time.

For a service emphasizing the crucifixion, you could feature a song service that utilizes the hymns of the cross. You could begin with "The Old Rugged Cross" and close with "In the Cross of Christ I Glory."

You could also feature hymns that focus on the life of Christ, leading up to the crucifixion. A hymn on the cross could precede the message.

IDEAS FOR THE SUNRISE SERVICE

Appropriate hymns can be selected and short talks can be given on the "morning after" theme. The topics would include "The Morning After the Betrayal" (How did Judas feel?), "The Morning After the Crucifixion" (How did the disciples feel?), "The Morning After the Resurrection," and "The Morning After the Second Coming."

If you have used the Tableau idea for Good Friday, and if someone played the part of Christ on the cross, have that same person appear at the Sunrise Service—alive and well!

You can easily put together a "first person" service with several individuals appearing in costume to tell their own story of the Passion Week events: Judas, the centurion, Peter, John, Simon of Cyrene, the soldiers who guarded the tomb, the women, Mary Magdalene, the two who went to Emmaus.

The morning of the Resurrection may be seen as one of the three great mornings of history. Appropriate music and a short talk can be given on "The First Morning" (Creation), "Resurrection Morning," and "The Last Morning" (2 Peter 1:19).

A SIMPLE SUNRISE SERVICE

"I WALKED TODAY WHERE JESUS WALKED"

Soloist: *Enters, wearing clothes similar to those worn by women in Jesus' day. She pauses and begins singing, "I Walked Today Where Jesus Walked." She takes a step or two, pauses, then repeats—all the while she is singing. She should be near her seat as she finishes singing.*

Narrator #1: *Enters from the same direction as the soloist only moments after she enters. He is wearing oriental garb, also. He steps to pulpit and watches and listens in a meditative manner. As soloist finishes and is seated, narrator rouses from meditative mood, turns, faces congregation, and speaks quietly but very distinctly.*

Narrator #1: I, too, have walked where Jesus walked. Each time that I am in Jerusalem at the Passover season, I go to the upper room. *(Begin playing "Break Thou the Bread of Life.")* There I see the Master as, on that memorable night, He took bread and blessed it and brake it and gave it to us and said, "Take, eat, this is my body." And He took the cup and gave thanks and gave it to us saying, "Drink ye all of it." How little we understood then what He meant when He said it was His blood of the New Testament that was shed for many for the remission of sins. Then we lifted our voices heartily and sang as we started out for the Mount of Olives.

I will never, as long as I live, forget that walk that night. The streets were dark as we made our way past the Temple. Although there were eleven disciples who were usually full of questions, we were all strangely quiet. No man spoke. Only the Master. *(Begin playing "Love Divine.")*

He told us about the vine and branches, that He is the TRUE vine, and we are the fruit-bearing branches. He said all who fail to bear fruit are cut off. He told us of the love between His Father and himself and of His love for us.

His voice was low and gentle as He said, "Greater love hath no man than this, that a man lay down his life for his friends." He said that we are His friends if we obey His commands. He then talked about the believer and the world—how the world would hate His followers and persecute them. He told us of the Comforter He would send.

Narrator #2:   *(Enters and stands beside Narrator #1.)*

We were amazed and could not understand when He told of His death, His resurrection, and His second coming.

Then there was that wonderful prayer! He prayed that the world might be one as He and His Father are One. *(Begin playing " 'Neath the Old Olive Trees.")*

After that, we crossed over the brook Kedron into the garden called Gethsemane. There He divided us into two groups and told us to watch while He went to pray. Oh, the anguish of the Master as He prayed alone that night! *(Stands thoughtfully during the music, " 'Neath the Old Olive Trees.")*

Duet: *"In the Garden" (vs. 1, 2)*

Organ: Chimes in the distance and the midnight hour begins to strike.

Choir: *" 'Tis Midnight" (vs. 3, 4), v. 3 all sing, v. 4 only men sing (singing melody not parts).*

Narrator #1: Oh, the agony of that night! The shame that burns within me to this day when I remember that we could not watch one hour with Him. We slept during His sorrow!

Then it was over. His will was completely surrendered to that of His Father. He was ready when Judas arrived with his kiss of betrayal. Jesus looked into the eyes of Judas and said, "Friend, wherefore art thou come?"

Then one of our number drew a sword and cut off the ear of a soldier. The Lord performed His last miracle of healing as He stopped, picked up the ear, and replaced it.

Narrator #2: Turning to the mob, He asked why they had come to take Him armed with swords and staves as if He were a thief. He told them that even then He could pray the Father and more than twelve legions of angels would come to rescue Him. *(Begin playing "Alone.")*

It seems I can hear them now as they leave the garden. The shouting, abusive soldiers leading our meek and humble Master. Truly, He was as a sheep being led to a slaughter—friendless and alone.

Solo: *Chorus of "Alone", very softly and distinctly, fading at last "alone."*

Narrator #1: Within the palace, the scribes and elders were assembled with Caiaphas, the high priest. He asked Jesus if He were the Christ, the Son of God. Jesus answered that He was and that later the high priest would see Him in His glory. Angered by this, the high priest charged Him with blasphemy. The council said He was guilty of death. The chief priests and all the council spit in His face. Some hit Him with their fists, while others slapped His face with their open hands.

It was about this time that Peter denied His Lord, with an oath.

Choir: *"Alone" chorus, softly.*

Narrator #2: When morning came, Jesus was bound and delivered to the governor, Pontius Pilate.

Narrator #1: Pilate suggested that they try Him according to their law, but they refused, saying it was not lawful for them to put a person to death. Pilate returned to Jesus and asked, "Art Thou the King of the Jews?" Jesus asked why he had asked this question. After Pilate answered, Jesus told him that His kingdom is not of this world, that if it were, His servants would fight to rescue Him.

Again, Pilate asked, "Art Thou a King, then?"

Jesus' reply was, "Yes, indeed, I am a King." He told Pilate that the reason He was born was to bear witness to the truth and that all who are of the truth listen to His voice.

Narrator #2: Now at the time of the Passover, it was custom for the governor to release a prisoner to the people. The chief priests and elders persuaded the multitude to demand the release of a notorious prisoner called Barabbas and put Jesus to death.

Pilate had the Master scourged. The Roman soldiers mocked Him by making a crown of thorns for His already torn and bleeding brow. They put a purple robe on Him. They slapped Him in the face with their hands and said, "Hail, King of the Jews."

Again, Pilate went before the people. This time he presented Jesus to them. He thought the sight of Him would touch their hearts. Here was the man who had healed their diseased bodies, brought sight to the blind, raised the dead, fed the hungry, and taught them all to love one another.

Here He stood before them—alone, humiliated, His body bruised and bleeding from the merciless beating.

Solo: *"Alone," v. 2; also chorus.*

Narrator #1: Pilate continued to seek a way to release Jesus; but after being threatened by the Jews, he released Him to them, and they led Him away. Our blessed Lord was forced to bear His own cross to the hill called Golgotha.

Choir: *"Must Jesus Bear the Cross Alone," v. 1.*

Narrator #1: Then they crucified the spotless Lamb of God, who never had known sin—with two thieves.

Choir: *V. 3, first line only, "Tell Me the Story of Jesus." (This is not intended as a 'special'; only as a thought provoking bit of background music. The word "pain" should be held and "faded" slowly.)*

Narrator #2: All are familiar with the story of our Lord on the cross. The terrible suffering, the humiliation, and in all of this—His thoughtfulness of His mother and His prayer for His murderers.

Organ: *Begin playing "The Old Rugged Cross."*

Narrator #2: After three hours of darkness, Jesus of Nazareth died.

Choir:	*"The Old Rugged Cross" (Chorus).*
Narrator #1:	Darkness reigned in our hearts and souls. Our disappointment was beyond compare. We were so sure this was the promised Messiah—and He was only a man, after all. A leader, yes. A truly great teacher, yes. A marvelous friend, yes. But only a man. And now, a dead man. Yes, our Leader was now dead and in the tomb of Joseph of Arimathea; and the Sabbath was at hand.
Choir:	*"Christ Arose", v. 1, 2, 3; chorus only after v. 3. (Solos by two different people for vs. 1 & 2, v. 2 by a man; v. 3 by all; also chorus)*
Narrator #2:	Yes! The Master did arise from the dead. Jesus of Nazareth became the Savior of the world and the Friend of all who believe.
Organ:	*Music begins, "I Walked Today Where Jesus Walked."*
Narrator #2:	Let us all walk today where Jesus walked—from our first steps in the earliest morning hours to our weary ones at night. Let us walk where the Master walked in love, in service to God and our fellow man, and in humility. Time and distance matter not. If we truly love Him and obey His commands, we are His and we walk with Him.
Choir:	*Softly, "I Walked Today Where Jesus Walked and Felt Him Close to Me"—end very softly.*